tecture

Cover design by Danielle Farmer.
Type set in Frutiger

ISBN: 978-0-7643-4848-8
Printed in China

Published by Schiffer Publishing, Ltd.
4880 Lower Valley Road
Atglen, PA 19310
Phone: (610) 593-1777; Fax: (610) 593-2002
E-mail: Info@schifferbooks.com

For our complete selection of fine books on this and related subjects, please visit our website at www.schifferbooks.com. You may also write for a free catalog.

This book may be purchased from the publisher. Please try your bookstore first.

We are always looking for people to write books on new and related subjects. If you have an idea for a book, please contact us at proposals@schifferbooks.com.

Schiffer Publishing's titles are available at special discounts for bulk purchases for sales promotions or premiums. Special editions, including personalized covers, corporate imprints, and excerpts can be created in large quantities for special needs. For more information, contact the publisher.

Andreas K. Vetter

designs for the contemporary garage

tecture

Schiffer
Publishing Ltd

4880 Lower Valley Road • Atglen, PA 19310

CONTENT

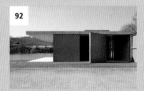

K+H HOUSE
Kunst+Herbert, Hamburg, Germany

MEIER/OLAVE HOME
Marein Gijzen and Daniel Gut, Zurich, Switzerland

47°40'28''N / 13°8'12''E HOUSE
Maria Flöckner and Hermann Schnöll, Salzburg, Austria

B IN K HOUSE
Matthias R Schmalohr, Bückeburg, Germany

KRE HOUSE
no. 555 – Takuya Tsuchida, Yokohama, Japan

MAISON ZUFFEREY
Nunatak Architectes Sarl, Fully, Switzerland

GRANGEGORMAN RESIDENCE
ODOS Architects, Dublin, Ireland

HOUSE IN SAIJO
Kazuyuki Okumura, Tokyo, Japan

HOME IN THE BERGISCHE LAND
Oxen + Partner Architekten, Hürth-Efferen, Germany

BASEMENT GARAGE UNDER THE MEADOW
Peter Kunz Architektur, Winterthur, Switzerland

O HOUSE
Philippe Stuebi Architekten, Zurich, Switzerland

VILLA 1
Powerhouse Company, Rotterdam, Netherlands

AATRIAL HOUSE
Robert Konieczny – KWK Promes, Katowice, Poland

FURNITURE HOUSE NO. 5
Shigeru Ban / Dean Maltz, New York, USA

HOUSE PM
S.O.F.A. Architekten, Vienna, Austria

GLASS PAVILION
Steve Hermann Design, Montecito, USA

VILLA F
Studio Martin Schroth, Rothenburg on the Tauber, Germany

HOUSE IN PETERSBERG
Sturm and Wartzeck, Dipperz, Germany

S/M/L HOUSE
Titus Bernhard Architekten, Augsburg, Germany

VILLA AT THE LAKE
Unger & Treina, Zurich, Switzerland

PREFACE

The intimate relationship between homeowners and their cars is well understood—and has been for the last 125 years. However, not many people think about the symbiosis between the house and the resident car. A difficult design challenge awaits architects who take on this task. Planning codes present obstacles, lot sizes often are small, and many homes require space for multiple vehicles. However, as the projects in this book show, innovative architectural solutions do not necessarily require a large budget.

This book explores the inventive ways architects have housed their clients' vehicles over the past decade with an international selection of forty homes in the mid to upper price ranges. Overly luxurious homes in exotic locations were mostly left out because of their special requirements. The entries represent diverse building shapes and suggest the infinite ways a house and lot can accommodate a car: with open parking, a garage under the building, a carport, an integrated garage, a separate garage, an underground garage, etc. Two functional aspects are particularly important: the parking space's relationship to the street, and its architectural connection to the house.

If clothing makes the man, as the saying goes, so does the house and car. The choice of whether to simply stow away your vehicle or present it with style is a personal one. However, the variety of options for doing so suggests that, with a bit of planning and design finesse, you can have an attractive place to park your ride.

THE GARAGE –
HISTORY AND CONCEPTS

After its invention in 1885, the automobile quickly became a luxury item—hence the first garages were successors to the carriage sheds of large mansions. But by the mid-twentieth-century, garages had become an essential part of domestic life, particularly in the United States, where the building of new highways resulted in bedroom communities that placed homes farther and farther from urban employment centers.

Throughout history, the most successful garages have been based on the design of the home. The old carriage house's main feature—the broad front entrance—is an obvious requirement, but the structure itself became a matter of style and taste, whether it related to a rustic country home, international modernism, or something else.

By the 1920s, for example, the European modernist movement's avant garde began stylizing the car as an indispensable accessory of the "new man." Le Corbusier's aim was to provide the optimal gear for the modern human: a house as a living machine ("machine à habiter"), including the automobile that swiftly and individually transports him to any destination. Le Corbusier's ideas are evident in one variation or another in this book: parking below the home, the pool on top of the garage, and the dynamic driveway. He created access to these elements playfully and masterfully: with exterior staircases, ramps, or formally differentiated paving strips on the front lawn—straight and double for the car, single and curvilinear for the owner.

After the late 1920s, the automobile was regarded as an essential part of the upscale home. It is interesting to observe the way cars were incorporated into different building forms. Walter Loos' orthogonal integration of garage and house is rather typical of this period; however, its formal integration into the floor plan is unusual. At the Villa Savoye, Le Corbusier's curved garage entrance echoes the house's rounded first floor, while one of Ludwig Mies van der Rohe's garages pushes into the rectangular house—a practical solution—and he bends the adjacent walls.

In addition to the garage, the roof and entrance driveways often require extensive designing, as traditionally they have been part of the socially important entrance areas of castle and villa architecture. Frank Lloyd Wright created early versions of these auto-centric entrances in his romantic prairie style, while the cigarette mogul Reemtsma's modernist villa in Hamburg featured its own gas station.

In Chicago, modernist architects Keck + Keck developed a distinctive combination of roofed driveway entrance and garage for a curved country home. George Fred Keck also created the "House of Tomorrow" presented in 1933 in Chicago, which housed the streamlined vehicle designed by Buckminster Fuller. If traveling by car was too slow, one could take the plane from the hangar tucked into the space below the terrace.

A few years into post-war Europe, modest single-family homes also got their own garage. By then, the automobile was already considered a standard feature of the American middle-class household. It was not unusual to see two cars parked in front of a single-family home

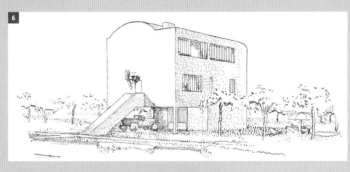

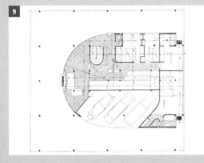

1 Josef Maria Olbrich, Glückert stable, Mathildenhöhe, Darmstadt, 1901–1905 | stable, carriage house for 3 carriages, chauffeur's apartment

2 Andrews, Jacques & Rantoul (Boston, USA), large garage for the villa of Mr. E.B. Dane, Boston, Massachusetts (USA), around 1905 + floor plan

3 Esselmann & Gerntke (Hamburg-Altona), garage Neumann home, Altona-Othmarschen, around 1925

4 Carl Weidemeyer (Ascona, Switzerland), garage Casa Rocca Vispo, Ascona (Switzerland), 1930

5 Walter Loos, Hillebrand house, Vienna (Austria), around 1932

6 Le Corbusier, design: Maison d'Artiste, 1922

7 Le Corbusier, project: Maison Canneel, Brussels (Belgium), 1929

8 Le Corbusier, Maison Cook, Boulogne sur Seine (France), 1926

9 Le Corbusier, Villa Savoye, Poissy (France), 1930 I floor plan + curved garage gate

with a pool, and they were used even for short distances. The general upswing of the 1950s saw the car as a supportive vehicle for a wide range of leisure activities.

During this period the Case Study houses were developed, following a solicitation by *Arts & Architecture* magazine. Architects designed thirty-six single-family homes between 1945 and 1966 with floor plans that accommodated one or several vehicles. These designed were quickly adopted internationally into the repertoire of modern residential architecture.

Professional photographs of the Case Study houses included the car and were widely published in lifestyle and home magazines. Not only did this experiment signal a movement toward modern design that drew inspiration from technology, it resulted in a new affinity for architect-designed homes.

A number of great model cars were featured in these photos, including Le Corbusier's vision car and the legendary Citroen DS by Peter Smithson. When Ernst Neufert published his "Bauentwurfslehre" (Building Design Treatise) in 1936, it was immediately accepted as a groundbreaking work about architecture, and the very first edition dealt with the vehicle as an integral part of the home. The solutions objectified the architecture and celebrated the low-maintenance characteristics of modern vehicles, compared to antique and vintage cars.

When the garage is conceived as a detached building, it can command as much attention as the house itself. There are many possible results: a box made from decorative concrete à la Neufert, a glazed pavilion by Mies van der Rohe, or a playful postmodern cube by Frank O. Gehry. Organic anthroposophical architecture

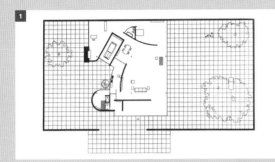

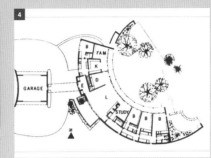

1 Ludwig Mies van der Rohe, House with Yard + floor plan, around 1934

2 Frank Lloyd Wright, Ward W. Willits House (Highland Park Illinois, USA), 1901–1903

3 Martin Elsässer, Villa Reemstma, (Hamburg-Othmarschen, Germany). 1930–1932

4 Keck & Keck, Milton Hirsh House (Highland Park, Illinois, USA), 1960 + floor plan

5 Ramey and Himes, model home of the National Association of Home Builders (Wichita, Kansas, USA), 1954

6 Craig Ellwood, Case Study House #18 (Beverly Hills, California, USA), 1956–1958

7 Pierre Koenig, Bailey House / Case Study House #21 (Los Angeles, USA), 1957–1959

8 Lina Bo Bardi, House Bardi (São Paulo, Brazil), 1951

9 George Fred Keck, House of Tomorrow, A Century of Progress International Exposition (Chicago, USA), 1933

reacts to this functional challenge and in the process finds its own form language.

Since then, our progressive, on-the-go lifestyles have created demand for inventive architecture that makes room for the auto, sports, and entertainment. This dream does not have to be as fantastical as a design by British architect Michael Webb, of the Archigram Group, in the early 1970s. In his drawing, the winged doors of a Lamborghini Countach are opened and the driver and passenger walk to the bedroom and bath on a nubbed path that resembles the gas pedal. The house is simply a dormant module and real life happens in the horse-power-laden sports car.

The concept shown next to it was more realistic: a car is driven into a cylindrical garage with a platform that turns and opens toward the living area, so you can step out of the car inside the house.

It's worth noting that when a home is designed in a progressive and analytical way, space for the car is more than an afterthought. NL Architects designed a house that curves outward, sheltering the car. su11 Architecture designed a ramp that leads from the car to a house made of multiple modules and materials. And a house by Actar Arquitectura features a parking pad on an incline under the house. It is similar to a parking platform that the firm MVRDV fitted into an Amsterdam townhouse.

Despite the availability of buses, railways, and subways, private cars continue to be the primary means of transit. Over the years, visionary architects and city planners have come up with futuristic responses to the proliferation of cars. As early as 1932, Frank Lloyd Wright wanted to do away with cities in favor of extensive settlements for "humans and their automo-

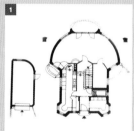

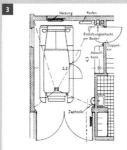
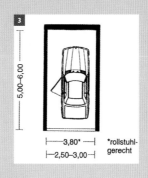

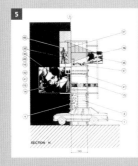
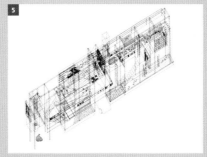

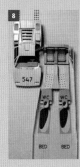
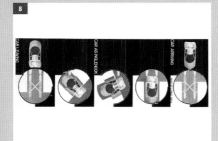
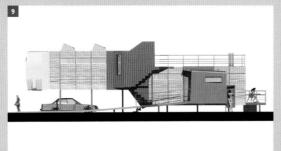

1 Christian Hitsch, House Eckart Hitsch (Salzburg, Austria), 1985 street view + first floor plan

2 Alison und Peter Smithson, Upper Lawn Pavilion (Wiltshire, Great Britain), 1959

3 Ernst Neufert, Bauentwurfs- lehre (Building Design Treatise), garage, first edition 1936/38 + edition 2005

4 Frank O. Gehry (Los Angeles, USA), Winton Guest House (Wayzata, Minnesota), USA, 1983–1987

5 Taeg Nishimoto (New York, USA), Projekt Plot House, published 1993 I section + organization system

6 James A. Speyer / David Haid, Rose Home, garage pavilion (Highland Park, Illinois, USA) 1953

7 NL architects (Amsterdam, Netherlands), Bendup Bendover, Bloemendaal, 2002

8 Michael Webb (London, Great Britain), study "his and hers house," study "Drive-in- Housing," mid-1970's

9 su11 Architecture & Design (New York, USA), Composite Housing, 1998–2000

bile." By 1958, however, he was dreaming of a "living city," with its inhabitants simply parking their helicopter-like vehicles on the terrace.

Planners have tried to realize these visionary ideas, too. Wes Jones' colorful village concept consisted of prefabricated house modules with minicars parking on top of the house and moving over the roofs like golf carts.

New materials and technology have the potential to transform architecture, introducing parking spaces that are both practical and theatrical. If your own garage is too dark and somber, you can add atmospheric light effects or—as in the case of a Herzog & de Meuron design for art collectors—video projections. NOX produced an entirely different effect years ago by using a biomorphic, dynamic system. The garage opening expands when two cars need to be parked.

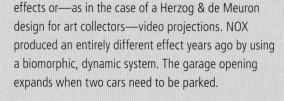

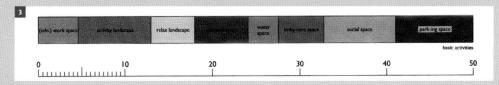

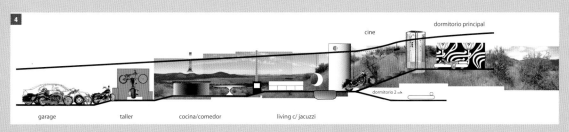

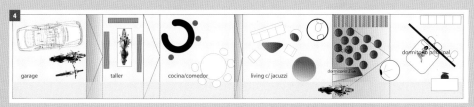

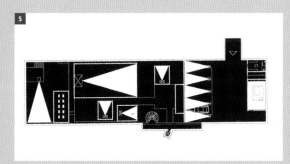

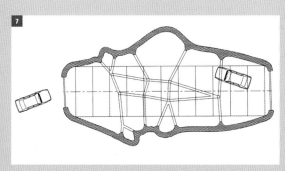

1 MVRDV (Rotterdam, Netherlands), house 12, Borneo-Sporenburg, Amsterdam 1996–2000, inner parking platform

2 Frank Lloyd Wright, "Living City," 1958

3 Actar Arquitectura (Barcelona, Spain), Paraloop, prototype for the Parasite Exhibition (Rotterdam, Netherlands), 2001, model + diagram

4 Supersudaka (Talca, Chile), Moto House (Talca, Chile), 2006

5 Herzog & de Meuron (Basel, Switzerland), Kramlich Residence (Napa Valley, California, USA), 1997, floor plan of lower floor

6 Wes Jones Partners (Los Angeles, USA), Silverlake por/con, Suburban Living, 2000

7 NOX (Rotterdam, Netherlands), OffTheRoad Speed, Eindhoven, 1999, floor plan + animation

ARCHITECTURAL
SOLUTIONS

Parking in front of the house

Even the simple act of parking in front of the house can be carried off elegantly. One solution is to use a parking-surface material that matches the building materials. The scope of architecture is visually enlarged and the parking space looks more valuable and deliberate when clearly distinguished from the street.

1 MMZ (Frankfurt at the Main (Germany), single-family home on a slope (Frankfurt at the Main), 2007.The mirror-image parking places, with their balustrade, read as a deliberate design gesture.

2 Peter Haimerl (Munich, Germany) conversion "The Black House," Krailling, 2005–06. The dark asphalt parking space visually merges with the house.

3 Akira Yoneda/Masahiro Ikeda-architecton (Tokyo, Japan), HP House, Meguro-ku, Tokyo, 2004. The house twists, creating the parking space.

Projecting roof

To avoid designing a separate small building that might not be approved by city planning authorities or that might encroach on the landscape, one solution is to extend a projecting roof over the entrance or side of the house. This provides rain-protected access to the car even where space is limited.

4 Archteam (Prag, Czech Republic), home, Kromeriz (Czech Republic), 2000. The most basic type of parking cover is achieved with a well-designed projecting roof.

5 Architectenbureau Paul de Ruiter (Amsterdam, Netherlands) Villa Berkel, 2004–2005. A small projecting roof grows logically from the building.

Volume cut

Pulling a lower section of the house inward eliminates the need for a proper garage. Here the outer wall becomes part of the parking area.

[1] Group A (Rotterdam, Netherlands), Villa (Bussum, (Netherlands), 2006–2008. Unique solution with a roofed driveway.

[2] Heide von Beckerath Alberts Architekten (Berlin, Germany), house in Wandlitz, 2001–2002. The incision provides access, natural light, and a place to park the car.

Lateral garage

The most convenient garage type allows access from the house's interior and provides a formally coherent outer appearance. Integrating a complementary garage volume can be an attractive solution.

[3] Rückert Architekten (Leichlingen-Witzhelden, Germany), extension House B, Solingen-Hästen, 2006. Cubical extension with kitchen and terrace on top of the double garage, flush-mount facing consisting of white enameled panels.

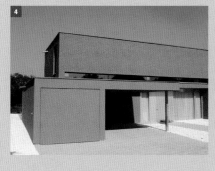

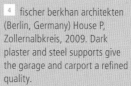

[4] fischer berkhan architekten (Berlin, Germany) House P, Zollernalbkreis, 2009. Dark plaster and steel supports give the garage and carport a refined quality.

[5] Walter Unterrainer. Atelier für Architektur (Feldkirch, Austria), House Ess-Längle (Vorarlberg, Austria), 2003–2004. Clad in black fleece and stainless steel bolts, the double garage blends with the house.

Parking under the building

The vehicle is housed beneath a protective overhang. The parking area's connection to the building is particularly important. In some examples, there is little room for secondary use.

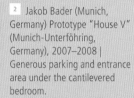

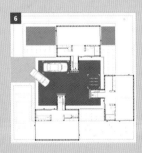

1 bolega + ehrhardt (Stuttgart, Germany), House S (multi-family house) (Ludwigsburg, Germany), 2002. Two inserted parking spaces flank the house entrance.

2 Jakob Bader (Munich, Germany) Prototype "House V" (Munich-Unterföhring, Germany), 2007–2008 | Generous parking and entrance area under the cantilevered bedroom.

3 LP Architektur (Altenmarkt, Austria) Haus Kramer (Radstadt, Austria), 2008–2010. Double carport in front of glazed entrance block.

4 Bolles & Wilson (Münster in Westphalia, Germany), Suzuki House (Tokyo, Japan), 1990. Parking in the extra space under the elevated house block.

5 Graser Architekten (Zurich, Switzerland) Studio house Huber (Lucerne-Emmenbrücke, Switzerland), 2001–2003. Spectacular supported building with large parking area.

6 Allmann Sattler Wappner (Munich, Germany) "Contemporary house" (Munich) 2003–2005. Layout with central parking space.

7 Allmann Sattler Wappner (Munich, Germany), "Contemporary house," Munich, 2003–2005. Open parking space under the module.

8 Sou Fujimoto (Tokio, Japan), House H (Tokyo, Japan), 2007-2009. Parking space in the open house block.

Garage house/garage box

A box-like garage works well with a cubical house, but whatever the form, it's important to choose a complementary building material. A well-designed detached garage conveys the automobile's emotional value and helps the property appreciate in value.

[1] Trint + Kreuder d.n.a. (Cologne, Germany), Home Strunk + Wenzel (Odenthal-Heidberg, Germany), 2006. Fair-faced concrete with formal adaption, intimate patio behind it.

[2] Fuchs Wacker Architekten (Stuttgart, Germany) Houses TDJ (Großheppbach, Germany), 2008 | Wood-paneled garage box forming a terrace.

[3] SoHo Architektur (Memmingen, Germany). House Bru 1.25 (Heimertingen, Germany), 2009. Gabled house and garage, fairfaced concrete box, stylistically an ideal duo.

[4] Franz Architekten (Vienna, Austria) EFH (Zellerndorf, Austria), 2009. Frontmost pavilion as a double garage, access, and storage room.

[5] Beat Rothen (Winterthur, Switzerland). Single-family home Hammerweg, Winterthur (Switzerland), 2001–2002. Nicely proportioned garage with blue-gray copper-titanium galvanized metal sheets.

[6] Nuno Brandão Costa (Porto, Portugal) House in Afife (Portugal), 2001–2004. Elaborately designed double garage with minimalist concept and material: black concrete and stainless steel sliding doors.

Parking on the roof

On a sloping site, a parking platform can be put on the roof, as long as there is a driveway connection. In addition to aesthetics, some issues to consider are water run-off and additional stress on the roof plate.

Integrated garage

Some living space is usually sacrificed when garages are attached to the house. One advantage, however, is that the house's architectural integrity is preserved. Furthermore, there is direct access to the house, and the garage can be heated efficiently.

1 AV 62 Arquitectos (Barcelona, Spain), Plentzia 63/64, Abanico de Plentzia (Bizkaia), 2001–2003. Colorful garage boxes on the house add a high recognition value.

2 Salvi Architecture (Delémont, Switzerland), Villa Montafon, Porrentruy (Switzerland), 2003–2005. A fully glazed entrance illuminates the double carport.

3 H Arquitectes (Sabadell, Barcelona, Spain), House Estrella/Casa 127 (Sabadell), 2003–2006. Double garage in a row on a very narrow layout.

4 Vaillo + Irigaray (Pamplona, Spain), Casa b2 (Pamplona), 2004–2005. Steel cladding adds visual interest to the gate and garage.

5 Gohm & Hiessberger (Feldkirch, Austria), House König (Feldkirch), 2000. The double garage's wooden gate slides to the side, providing privacy for the pool. In lieu of a basement, a large storage area is located to the right of the garage.

6 Synn Architekten (Wien, Austria), House Elise (Vienna), 2007–2009. A glazed sectional garage door illuminates the corner next to the entrance.

7 Dirk Jan Postel (Rotterdam, Netherlands), House van der Meulen (Almelo, Netherlands), 1996–1997. House block entirely made from glass panels, masterful treatment of the illumination including the garage.

Dominant garage

Where space allows, garages can celebrate the car with inventive materials and unusual forms appropriate to the house or site. Even if parking is a secondary factor when planning the home, it should not be disregarded. A car is an important means of transportation, and in many cases the owner's pride and joy. Why not honor it with appropriate shelter?

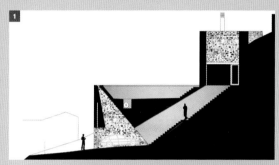

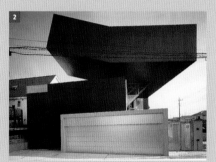

1 Markus Wespi Jérôme de Meuron Architekten (Caviano / Zurich, Switzerland), Holiday home (Brione, Switzerland), 2005. Block-like garage with cobblestone facing, cleverly integrated skylight and pool + section.

2 Akira Yoneda/Architecton + Masahiro Ikeda (Tokyo, Japan),
"White Base" home with studio (Kodaira, Tokyo), 2002–2006. Obliquely fitted garage box for a car collection + floor plan.

3 Architekturbüro Früh (Hard, Austria) House O (Lustenau, Austria), 2007. Basement garage with a long driveway and light-reflective copper enclosure.

4 Kanner Architects (Santa Monica, California, USA) 511 House (Pacific Palisades, California), 2001. Large exposed garage with high translucent gate.

Carport

Carports have the advantage of being lightly built and less prominent, which often makes permitting easier. They also lend themselves to inventive forms and unusual materials.

1 Hellriegel Architekten (Cologne, Germany) Home H (Cologne), 2005. Carport as the entrance arc with integrated bell, mailbox, and storage.

2 LP Architektur (Altenmarkt, Austria) House Kaiser (Goldegg, Austria), 2005–2007. Geometrically purified concrete carport with lateral and rear access.

3 Jan Jonkers (Zeist, Netherlands) Carport (Bloemendaal, Netherlands), 2003–2004. The dark rear storage room contributes to the illusion of the hovering roof slab.

4 LIN (Berlin, Germany) House OHK (Oldenburg), 2002–2003. Carport as a half barrel made from galvanized sheet metal.

5 VMX Architects (Amsterdam, Netherlands), Irish embassy (Wasenaar, Netherlands), 2007. Combination of projecting roof and carport, L-shaped steel plate construction.

6 Sou Fujimoto (Tokyo, Japan), House NA (Tokyo), 2011. Integration of the carport into the steel support structure.

Thoroughfare

A thoroughfare requires sufficient space behind and in front of the house. It makes sense to use thin building materials to minimize the space requirements. In addition to a roofed parking space, it also accommodates a second vehicle, a trailer, or a place to do maintenance work.

1 EM2N (Zurich, Switzerland) Heaven and Earth: Peak Villa (Ordos Project) (Ordos, Inner Mongolia, China), 2007–2008 | Round passage/driveway/garage.

2 Stéphane Beel (Gent, Belgium) Villa "G," 2006. Passage with large carport.

3 k_m.architektur (Bregenz, Austria) House Eberle-Böhler, (Wolfurt, Austria), 2001–2002. The cut-out thoroughfare is formally integrated into the architecture.

Underground garage

An underground garage is the most elaborate solution from a construction standpoint. Yet it also gets cars out of the way. In addition to a ramp, a garage in the basement or set into a slope must have room for maneuvering. Lower-lying garages also require heating and, more importantly, ventilation. It is common for underground garages—particularly those set deep into the ground—to include a passenger elevator.

4 Bearth & Deplazes Architekten (Chur, Switzerland) Single-family home in Riler-Gey (Eschen, Liechtenstein), 2003–2004. Underground garage with subterranean passageway.

5 LH Architekten (Hamburg, Germany), House T (Osnabrück), 2010. Inconspicuous, integrated underground garage.

Staged garage

An elaborate, staged garage is a display space, though it is usually not entered by people who are not part of the family. A glass wall is often used to allow views inside while keeping the car behind closed doors, as demonstrated in some of the Case Study houses of the mid-twentieth century.

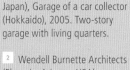

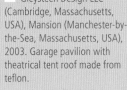

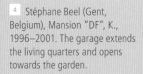

1 Jun Igarashi (Hokkaido, Japan), Garage of a car collector (Hokkaido), 2005. Two-story garage with living quarters.

2 Wendell Burnette Architects (Phoenix, Arizona, USA), Burnette House (Sunnyslope, Arizona, USA), 1988–1995. Generous carport under the house with floor lights reminiscent of a runway.

3 Gleysteen Design LLC (Cambridge, Massachusetts, USA), Mansion (Manchester-by-the-Sea, Massachusetts, USA), 2003. Garage pavilion with theatrical tent roof made from teflon.

4 Stéphane Beel (Gent, Belgium), Mansion "DF", K., 1996–2001. The garage extends the living quarters and opens towards the garden.

5 Seth Stein Architects (London, Great Britain), conversion of carriage house (London), 1997. Tiny double garage with elevator which shows off the car in the dining room. When the parking platform is raised the lower floor can be used as living space.

6 Holger Schubert/Archisis (Los Angeles, USA), Home superstructure (Los Angeles), 2006–2007.Living room with a parking space for a Maserati; an elevator platform allows the vehicle to roll out before starting the engine.

7 Mutsue Hayakusa / Cell Space Architects (Tokyo, Japan), House in Motoazabu (Tokyo), 2000–2002. The car has its own glazed and mirrored round room, despite the small living space.

Car elevator

A special cargo elevator or a tight-fitting elevator platform makes it easy to park the vehicle in an underground garage, eliminating space-consuming entrances. For high-end apartments downtown, parking in front of the door or on a private loggia is another elegant and safe solution. This is also ideal for an electric charging station.

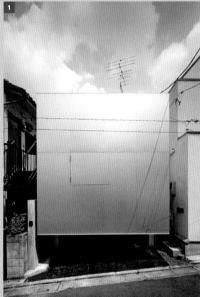

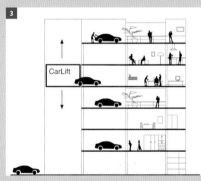

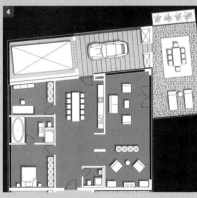

1 spacespace (Osaka, Japan), Lang Tall House, Meguro-ku (Tokyo), 2006. The house's slab facade functions as a spectacular garage gate that rises and lowers on cue.

2 Manfred Dick (Berlin, Germany), CarLoft (Berlin), 2006–2009. Apartment with parking space in the loggia, car elevator for vehicle and occupants.

3 CarLoft. Driver, passenger and baggage are brought to the home entrance without getting out of the car.

4 CarLoft. A clever layout puts the carport comfortably next to the apartment.

Custom solutions

Just as the garage developed from carriage sheds, barns, and workshops, today it is still very much connected to production, storage, and technology. One homeowner combines the garage with a hobby workshop, while the garage by x architekten reflects the traditional farmhouse layout with a main garage and secondary building. Manufacturers have developed clever solutions that turn the act of parking into an experience.

1 Harrison Architects (Seattle, USA), Green Roof Workshop (Kirkland, Washington), 2003. Freestanding garage with workshop for furniture making, canted grass roof.

2 x architekten (Vienna, Austria), Home "The small black one,"(Gunskirchen, Austria), 2010. A carport connects the garage with accessory storage.

3 Drehplatte 505 (Fa. Wöhr, Friolzheim, Germany). A platform turns the car electronically, optimizing a small space.

4 Parklift 462 (Fa. Wöhr, Friolzheim, Germany). The covered lift provides a seamless, low-profile option for a carport.

FUTURE

The public is increasingly aware that fossil fuels used in cars and homes harm the environment. Many architects are dedicated to designing energy-neutral buildings that at times include the vehicle. The Danish architectural firm PQL Studio is a leader in this area. Its decidedly futuristic homes make the most of wind and solar energy. A hybrid car docked at the carport gets its hydrogen supply while supporting the energy requirements of the house with its energy cell. This concept is already a reality at the Swedish One Tonne Life House, with its active-energy carport. In the future, such a carport could be tied into an expansive interregional smart grid and provide surplus power. If electric carport stations were connected with each other, both city and rural areas could contribute to ecologically sound energy production.

1 Plus-Energiehaus research team of the Technical University Darmstadt, 2010 (Jo Eisele, Jens Schneider), Plus-Energiehaus, Project 2010.Parking space and charging station for the electric vehicle in the "energy garden."

2 Designed by Ken Sakamura (Tokyo, Japan), TRON Toyota Dream House PAPI, Nagakute (Aichi, Japan), 2004. Prefabricated high-tech home with garage and charging station with energy recovery.

3 Gert Wingårdh (Gothenburg, Sweden), One Tonne Life House, Serienhaus von A-Hus (Hässleby/ Stockholm), 2011. Solar carport for home and electric vehicle.

4 PQL Studio (Copenhagen, Denmark), Project Producer, 2011. Plus-energy home with carport gas station.

5 SIEMENS AG, Energiefluss Haus, Flexible Stromflüsse, 2010. HaussusussHome and vehicle contain elements of the smart grid.

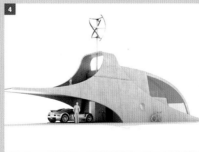

HOME & AUTO
40 INTERNATIONAL PROJECTS

LITTLE BROTHER

Hellmuth House

This quintessential German home is situated at the edge of a small town with a view of the fields, lagoons, and forests, and trees dotting a manicured lawn. The charmingly self-assured design followed the local building code: light-colored plaster finish, steeply angled roof, and high jamb walls. Its interpretation resulted in a visually pleasing building with clean contours, minimal roof overhangs, large windows, upright dormers, and a sleek galvanized roof. The garage, however, plays a singular role in the overall composition. It consists of its own proper building, which has moved in like a relative right in front of the main building. 03 Architekten solved the problem of street-facing parking playfully and economically. Not only is the car tucked behind a handsome gate, the garage door echoes the shape and materials of the home's openings. The garage's high roof allowed for a multi-purpose room under the gable, accessible via an external staircase.

ARCHITECT:
03 Architekten,
Munich (Germany)

LOCATION:
Eichenau (Germany)

COMPLETION:
2005

TYPE:
Dominant garage

VEHICLES:

A small exterior staircase (added after the photo was taken) leads to the attic room over the garage.

The front view is an optical illusion: the garage volume is actually significantly lower than the main house behind it.

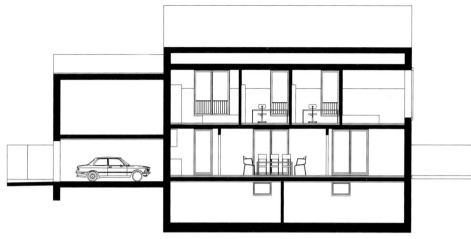

Section
scale 1:200

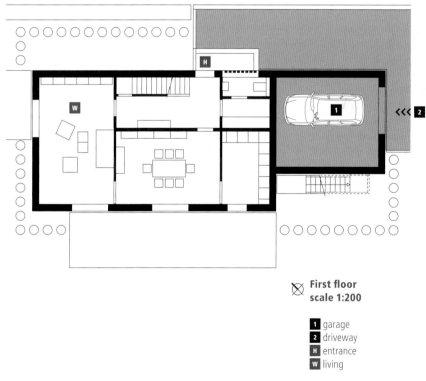

First floor
scale 1:200

1 garage
2 driveway
H entrance
W living

The house and attached garage
share a roofing, siding, and window
vocabulary, creating a cohesive look.

COOL AND COMPLEX

Architect and Artist's House

ARCHITECT:
Andreas Fuhrimann,
Gabrielle Hächler
Architekten, Zurich
(Switzerland)

LOCATION:
Zurich-Uetliberg
(Switzerland)

COMPLETION:
2004

TYPE:
Integrated garage

VEHICLES:

This monolithic, polygonal building is tucked into a hill close to a forest overlooking Zurich. The fact that neither its floor plan nor its front and rear side are immediately apparent hint at its complex design and program, which incorporates four apartments. Fuhrimann and Hächler solved the challenges so successfully that, after completion, images of the gray concrete home immediately began appearing in industry publications. The most prominent photographs featured a sporty car parked in front of the building, with its galvanized sheet-metal panels and sleek windows (see book cover). The photograph gives the impression that the car has just rolled out under the futuristic garage door, consisting of two glazed gates with horizontally perforated metal plates. Passing through the recessed entrance, one enters a two-story foyer. Unfinished concrete, pine wood, and galvanized steel help to spatially differentiate the two duplexes and two top-floor apartments. The basement, staircases, and dividing walls were made from concrete, while ceilings and room walls are clad in wood panels. While the rear facade opens onto the south garden; its front facade faces north toward the city below.

The house's garden-side view reveals its complexity.

This house's success is based on a strong design that seamlessly incorporates the garage.

**Front
scale 1:200**

Site plan

Frameless windows
dematerialize toward the view
of Zurich.

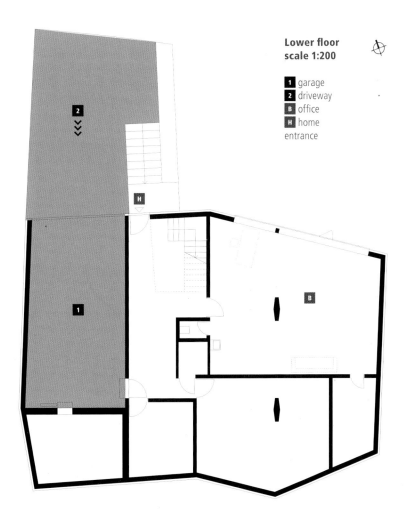

**Lower floor
scale 1:200**

1 garage
2 driveway
B office
H home
entrance

In contrast to its massive base,
the home's edges are
generously glazed.

Entrance and garage gate are in
keeping with the home's
industrial look.

ASYMMETRIC CHARM

Zeimer House

This small home is a hallmark of AFF Architekten's work: a clear and distinctive shape, a functional floor plan, and that "special something." Local building and design codes predetermined the house and roof's essential features, based on typical homes of the 1920s, and as is common, the limited lot size collided with the clients' wish for an external garage and storage buildings. To accommodate the program, the home's second floor was simply pulled forward about 2.5 meters (8.2 feet). The move had two effects: The resulting asymmetry makes the house look more dynamic. And the upper bedroom level gained two

useful storage and wardrobe rooms, plus a spacious central staircase with a library-style study lit by a floor-level window. Three generations share these rooms, so the extra living area is a bonus. The second floor's cubed pop-up volume helps to define the entrance through the two glass doors. Two cars can be parked here and loaded and unloaded while protected from rain, and the owners can sit outside under the roof. Gravel pathways and parking spaces absorb rainwater from the roof while creating a transition between the house and garden.

ARCHITECT:
AFF Architekten, Berlin (Germany)

LOCATION:
Berlin-Kleinmachnow (Germany)

COMPLETION:
2006

TYPE:
Volume cut

VEHICLES:

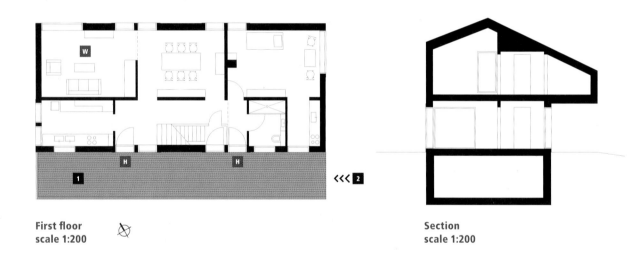

First floor
scale 1:200

<<< 2

1 parking
2 driveway
H entrance
W living

Section
scale 1:200

Symbiotic design:
"The house's shape articulates an empty space around the automobile. When the car is absent this space looks awkward: the balance between home and mobility is disturbed."
(Robert Zeimer)

OAK AND CONCRETE

Hexahedron House

ARCHITECT:
Architekturbüro Stocker,
Remshalden (Germany)

LOCATION:
Engelsbrand (Germany)

COMPLETION:
2009

TYPE:
Integrated garage

VEHICLES:

The tower-like gray house in the Black Forest south of Pforzheim is at the core of a small arcadian complex of buildings and gardens. Over the years, the owners (under the name of Topoi Engelsbrand) commissioned several thematic pavilions, a pool, and a flat-roofed building with a brook flowing through the open center. Its latest addition is the house, whose concrete facade and geometric template give it a distinct presence. The architects paid special attention to the quality of surfaces and the relationship between surface and opening. Rock-like, yet purposefully artificial, the house is set into the wild cultivated landscape and brings to mind Emil Kaufmann's term "autonomous architecture." The lower floor reflects the tradition of the early Italian Renaissance villa with its demonstrative reticence. The only opening in the concrete wall is the garage gate fitted with untreated oak boards. Above it, broad two-floor-high window panes reveal the home's interior volume. The large garage has space for two additional small antique cars. Straight and curved staircases lead from the terrace upward through the living quarters and upper bedrooms. Driving onto the lot, the car follows the compound's main axis, which is oriented toward the solstice.

Bright and airy rooms flow inside the heavy outer walls.

An oak tree on the property supplied the material for the garage gate.

Site plan

Section
scale 1:200

The driveway follows a solstice line that runs through the property.

Lower floor
scale 1:200

1 garage
2 driveway

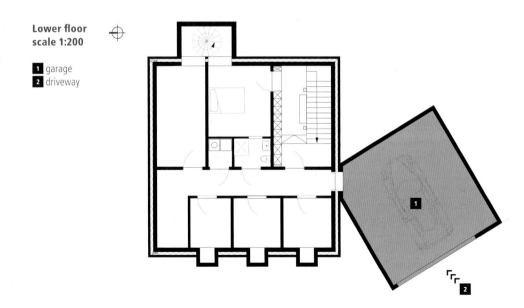

The house's presence
dominates the landscape.

ANGLE OF REPOSE

Reflection of Mineral

Tokyo architects are accustomed to designing homes on small lots, such as this 3.70 x 5.15-meter-lot (12 x 17 feet) in the Nakano district. They know how to squeeze value out of every inch of building space in the Japanese megalopolis. Their European and American colleagues, initially astonished by such images and floor plans, have long since become accustomed to the craftiness with which the Japanese fit almost any program into a minimal volume, particularly since the 1990s. Contrary to what one might expect, the homes are much more than crowded boxes. This four-story building was planned around the concepts of mineral and reflection. The concrete building, fitted onto a corner, is based on frame construction and window walls. The desire to provide varied sunlight exposure led to a polyhedral shape with folded walls, resulting in an interior quasi-twisting space of 44.62 square meters (146 square feet). The little house, equipped with under-floor heating and air conditioning, features a central living room window that seems to look toward the big city. The architects succeeded in fitting a building with maximum area onto a small lot and incorporating a clever roofed parking space. The head-turning sight of a round VW Beetle parked under the home's folded walls has made it one of the most-photographed contemporary buildings in Japan.

ARCHITECT:
Atelier Tekuto, Tokyo (Japan)

LOCATION:
Tokyo (Japan)

COMPLETION:
2006

TYPE:
Volume cut

VEHICLES:

The sculptural home reacts to the aesthetic chaos of the Japanese city.

The interior develops as a cohesive space shaped like the outer wall.

A curvaceous car contrasts with the house's thorough formality.

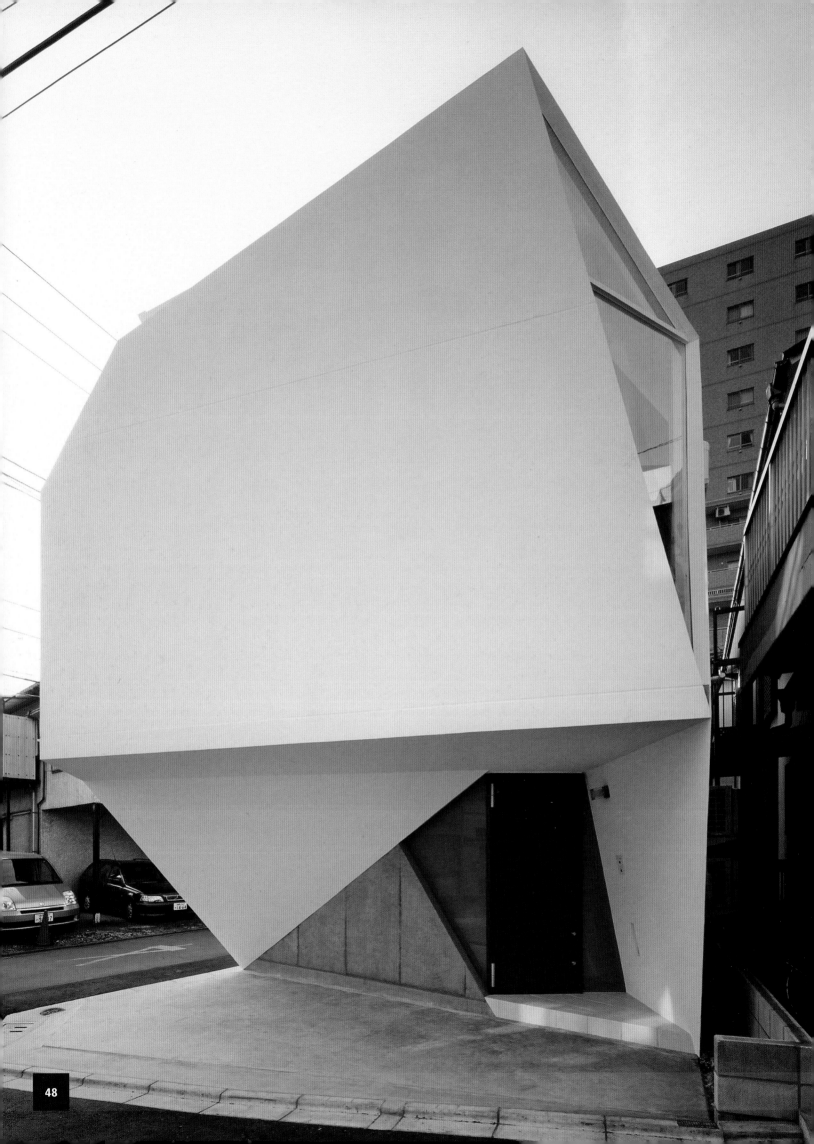

City views and light flow in through the facade's prominent rectangular window.

Site plan

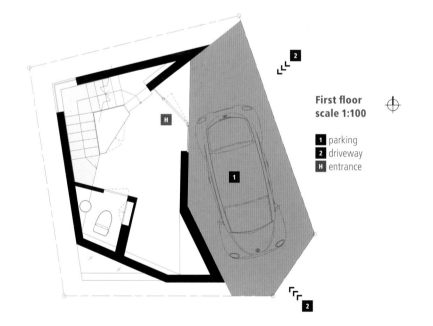

First floor
scale 1:100

1 parking
2 driveway
H entrance

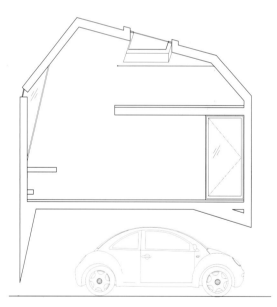

Section
scale 1:100

The inventively shaped house creates a covered parking niche on a tiny lot.

ALPINE HOUSE ABSTRACTED

MMN House

ARCHITECT:
Bonnard Woeffray
Architectes, Monthey
(Switzerland)

LOCATION:
Collombey (Switzerland)

COMPLETION:
2007

TYPE:
Carport

VEHICLES:

On the hills around Collombey, a small Swiss village in the Unterwallis area southeast of Lake Geneva, chalet-style houses are typical. But not every house has wooden timbers and a broad gabled roof. The MMN house goes against convention even though it is contextual; the architects have reduced the vernacular alpine style to its essence. The snow-shedding roof angle and the wood siding (black-glazed spruce) has been retained, along with the abstracted chalet-like volume. Bonnard and Woeffray created a polygonal box that is hermetically closed—entirely without windows—on the side facing the hill. On the other, a corner has been eliminated in favor of a sun-facing loggia. One of the particular qualities of the regional building style, taking advantage of the sloping hillside for a fantastic view of the valley and the Alps, has been developed by using large fixed window panes that provide light and views of the bright, uncluttered interior. The color orange is the central motif of this successful crossover style, in which the pastoral landscape meets a provocatively artificial urban aesthetic. The front carport picks up on this concept and shows it off in an orange trapezoidal opening that welcomes the vehicle.

An iconic Alps panorama surrounds the kitchen like a wall-to-wall photograph.

The carport's intense interior color is repeated on the loggia.

Site plan

The carport's trapezoidal layout reflects the home's silhouette.

**Section
scale 1:200**

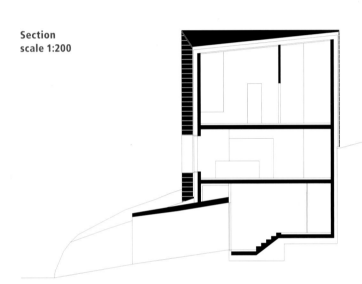

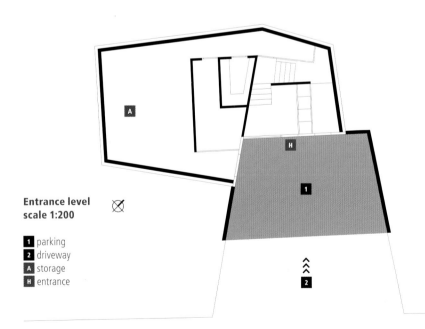

**Entrance level
scale 1:200**

1 parking
2 driveway
A storage
H entrance

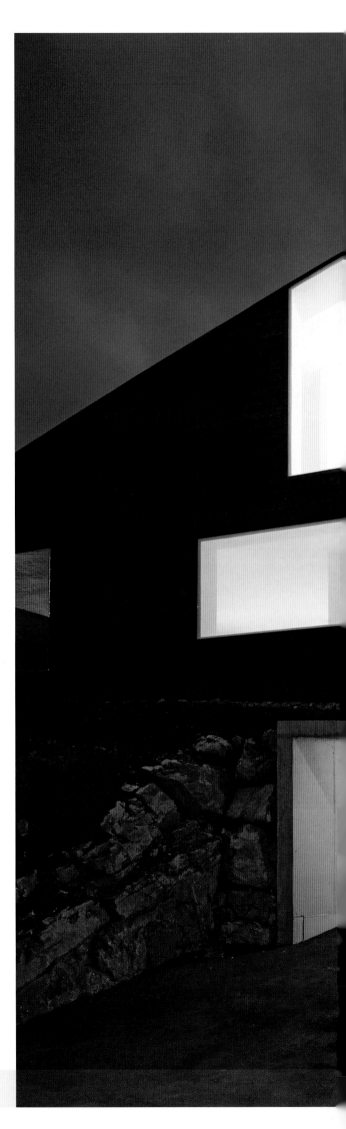

REDUCTIVIST THINKING

Mountain House

The small single-family house, on the Swabian Alps in Waldstetten, reflects an expert's handling of materials, details, and execution. Conceived as a modernist two-story box, the home's economical floor plan includes three bedrooms, two bathrooms, and a hallway with built-in cabinets on the top floor. Basement rooms are pushed into the hillside so that the living and kitchen areas can claim the premium south-facing exposure and connection to the terrace.

Located close to the entrance, the gangway-style staircase seems to have been lowered from the ceiling like a white lacquered box. Clad in brown-gray mineral plaster, the simple box features closed walls and windows exactly where they are needed. Its understated front facade includes a vertically divided garage gate and a metal entry door with a matt finish.

ARCHITECT:
C18 Architekten, Stuttgart (Germany)

LOCATION:
Waldstetten-Wissgoldingen (Germany)

COMPLETION:
2006

TYPE:
Integrated garage

VEHICLES:

The simple, unornamented building and taut materials reflect modernist principles.

Good things take time. While the collector's car could be called a classic, the tree will have to wait a few more years.

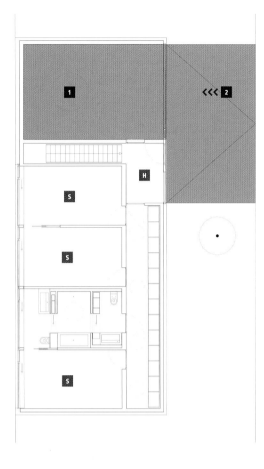

**Entrance level
scale 1:200**

1 garage
2 driveway
H entrance
S bedroom

The bedrooms lie behind the opaque front facade and are reached by way of an elegant hallway with reflective walls and skylights.

High-quality materials belie the plaster-clad home's simple form. The garage sits flush right of the glossy front door.

CLASSICS BEHIND GLASS

T-Bone House

ARCHITECT:
Coast Office
Architecture,
Stuttgart (Germany)

LOCATION:
Waiblingen (Germany)

COMPLETION:
2006

TYPE:
Integrated showroom
garage

VEHICLE:

This single-family home for four inhabitants gets its name from the wood siding that wraps the building in a T-shape. Situated above the Rems Valley and surrounded by low-density neighborhoods, it stands on a block-like concrete base whose generous depth supports the narrower second and third floors. The broad driveway platform sits on the lot's upper slope. Bedrooms are housed on the top floor, while the dining room, kitchen, study, and ground floor living space are downstairs and divided into three bays. A central entrance connects two corner rooms that are glazed on three sides—the living room on the west and the "living-garage" on the east, where a red 1974 Porsche 911 Targa is parked. This room—fitted with a heated slate floor, curtains, and leather-covered wall cupboards—honors the car and also functions as an occasional playroom. This kind of "inside parking" is particularly attractive at night, when the garage reads as an illuminated shrine. The generously proportioned, easily accessible room could be repurposed as an additional bedroom or living space.

It is hard to imagine a more living-room-like garage.

When you integrate the vehicle into the residence this completely, you risk the possibility that it will participate in family reunions.

The car takes pride of place in its own glass box.

Site plan

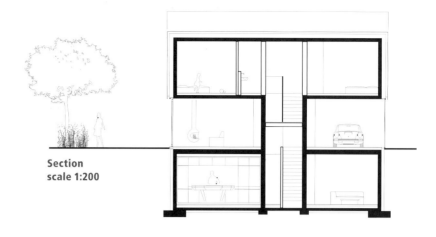

**Section
scale 1:200**

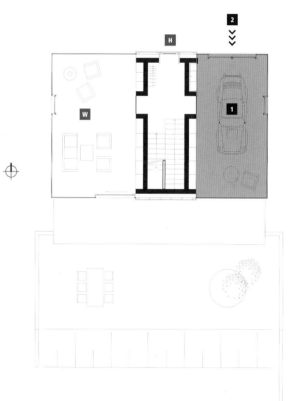

**First floor
scale 1:200**

1 garage
2 driveway
H entrance
W living area

The architecture-auto affinity is
particularly noticeable at dusk.

The multifunctional glass room also can be used as a living room.

STACKED DECK

Crepain Spaens House

The classic townhouse, with its vertical floor plan, offers the advantage of close proximity to shopping, restaurants, cultural events, and transportation. Those amenities attracted the owners of this 4 x 12-meter (13 x 39-foot) Antwerp townhouse. Its four-floor layout reflects the neighboring historic buildings; however, the new split-level reconfiguration made room for an elevator and a central sky-lighted staircase. The architect inserted asymmetrical glass panes into the dark-colored facade, whose abstracted bays recall those of traditional townhouses. A ground-floor curtain wall puts the owner's car on prominent display. This area's semi-public character evokes the modern atrium-style home or early castle gateways, while playfully manipulating stairwell access. In addition to the parking space, the multipurpose room combines accessibility, storage, and a laundry.

ARCHITECT:
CSD Architecten,
Antwerp (Belgium)

LOCATION:
Antwerp (Belgium)

COMPLETION:
2009

TYPE:
integrated garage

VEHICLES:

**First floor
scale 1:100**

1 garage
2 driveway
H entrance
M multipurpose room

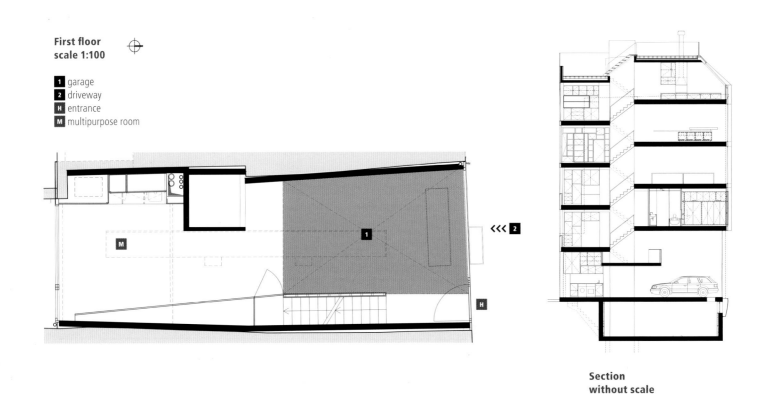

**Section
without scale**

At night, the city house and
garage become transparent.

FAMILY CONNECTION

Guido Dongus House

ARCHITECT:
Dongus Architekten,
Leonberg (Germany)

LOCATION:
Leonberg (Germany)

COMPLETION:
2003

TYPE:
Integrated showroom
garage

VEHICLES:

This eye-catching architect's home is one of two residential buildings joined in a V-shape. It is located in northern Stuttgart, overlooking fruit and wine plantations and not far from the famous interstate tunnel on A 81. One can't help but appreciate the location's automotive affinity, as Zuffenhausen and Weissach (Porsche's research center and headquarters) are stationed close by. The architect and owner specified a facade pattern consisting of glass and folded bands of pre-manufactured steel concrete. Open curtains reveal living spaces sparsely furnished with ceiling-high built-in cabinets and walnut shelves. Sliding doors give the open floor plan flexibility, and glass curtain walls present the car in a showroom-like setting.

**Top floor
scale 1:250**

1 garage
2 driveway
s bedroom

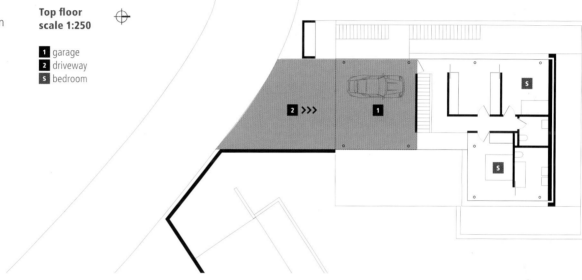

The car makes itself
at home in
showroom style.

DOUBLE UP

Garage and Carport

Drewes+strenge provided two separate parking areas at this German home. Entered from the driveway, the double garage is a basic box made from cast-in-place concrete with drainage at the rear wall. Behind it, the flat roof of a double carport is used as a balcony outside the children's playroom. A square matt glass brick wall and bamboo hedge provide privacy and climate protection, and an outer staircase made from galvanized sheet metal connects the rooftop to the garden. While the main garage sits on a smooth asphalt platform, cobblestones mark the transition point between the carport and the lawn. Other textural materials include Corten steel at the entryway and a firewood-like wall behind the carport. The result is an attractive landscape for leisure activities, children's play, and several vehicles belonging to three generations of an active family.

ARCHITECT:
drewes+strenge architekten, Berlin/ Herzebrock/ San Francisco

LOCATION:
Oelde-Lette/Westphalia (Germany)

COMPLETION:
2005

TYPE:
Garage and carport

VEHICLES:

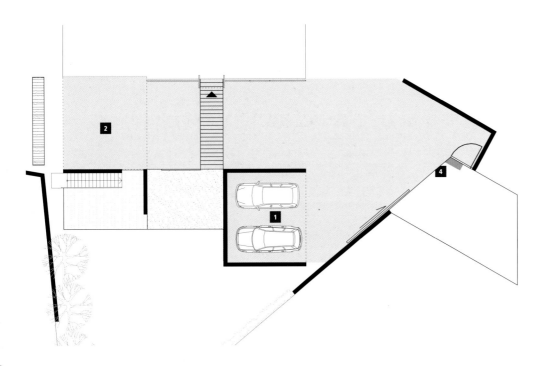

First floor scale 1:250

1 garage
2 carport
3 parking
4 driveway

Site plan

The concrete garage and carport, Corten steel entryway, and larch wood siding will be attractive even after many years.

BOARD ROOM

Woodpile Garage

ARCHITECT:
Elke Reichel
Architekten GmbH,
Stuttgart/Marienberg
(Germany)

LOCATION:
Marienberg/Erz moun-
tains (Germany)

COMPLETION:
2009

TYPE:
Garage box

VEHICLES:

Commissioned to build a double garage in the southern Saxony town of Marienberg, Stuttgart architect Elke Reichel took advantage of the forests of this low mountain range, purchasing renewable lumber for a low price nearby. Once a carpentry workshop had built five sections from boards of varying widths—treated and then nailed and bolted together—the garage was mounted on a concrete platform in one day. The extensively planted flat roof is sealed with two layers of tar paper. While the boards were smoothed on the inside, the outside was left natural and uneven in keeping with their origins, and the edges interlock. No two boards are the same age and each has weathered differently, adding to the striped effect. The decidedly architectural dark metal door provides an appealing counterpoint.

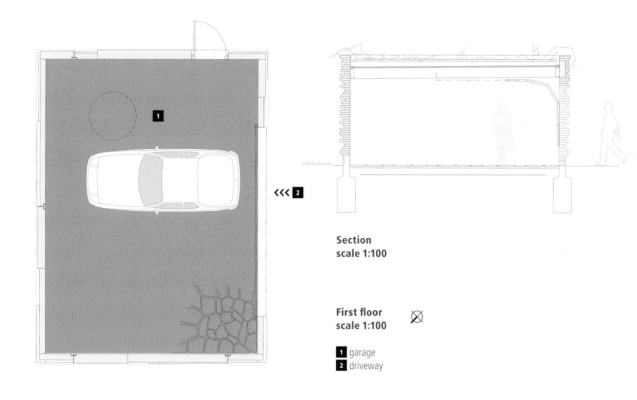

**Section
scale 1:100**

**First floor
scale 1:100**

1 garage
2 driveway

Snow on the boards underscores their natural origins, and the raw material dissolves the barrier between domesticity and nature.

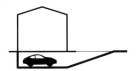

POLISHED UNDERPASS

Casa del Atrio

ARCHITECT:
Fran Silvestre Arquitectos, Valencia (Spain)

LOCATION:
Urbanización Santa Bárbara, Godella, Valencia (Spain)

COMPLETION:
2010

TYPE:
Underground garage

VEHICLES:

Casa del Atrio, designed by Fran Silvestre Arquitectos in the firm's hometown of Valencia, combines reductivist Mediterranean architecture with the horizontality of a Mies van der Rohe. Positioned on the squarish lot's western and southern edges, the L-shaped house sprawls around the swimming pool and an enormous terrace that inspired the project's name. Visitors enter on the opposite side on a narrow pathway that runs along the living wing. The owners approach their home by car in this hot climate and asked for a parking area that would not heat up in the sun—hence the illumi-nated ramp at the property's northern edge that leads down to the four-car subterranean garage. The driveway, maneuvering space, and connection to the living quarters, via a wide sliding door at the main staircase, are of generous size, and the lighting and surface materials do not distinguish between the above-ground and underground rooms. The lower floor plan offers an experience in every direction—library, gym, wine cellar, or the parking hall with its automotive gems.

A strip of light guides arriving vehicles into the garage. The house entrance is on the opposite side.

View from the lower floor into the underground garage. The driveway's light strip is visible through the open sliding door.

A trench-like terrace along the pedestrian entrance scoops light into the rooms on the lower floor.

The subterranean garage has indirect soffit lighting.

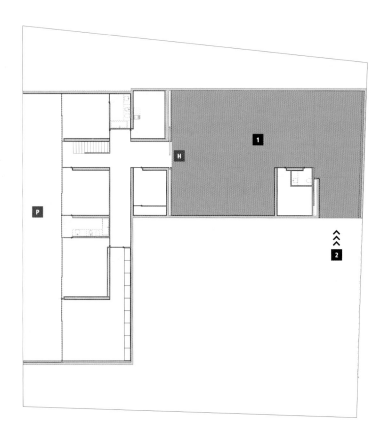

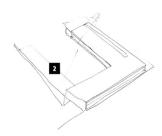

**Lower level
scale 1:350**

1 garage
2 driveway
H entrance
P patio

At night the underground garage becomes a minimalist light sculpture.

BOXED SET

Rupp Loft

This home's dark skeleton consists of double T-girders that allowed a remarkably open framework. Everything rests on four columns, like the original version of this concept, the Farnsworth house by Mies van der Rohe. The estuarine area of the New Rhine river southeast of Lake Constance presents a possibility of flooding, which required the home to be raised on stilts. Architect Alexander Früh inserted the living area like a box into the supporting skeleton. Almost 100 square meters (328 square feet), the one-bedroom floor plan features flowing living quarters opening toward the garden via a floating porch, which also contains the entryway. The interior of this "machine à habiter" features detailed installations including a kitchen, the living area, cooking, dining, and the bedroom. A low horizontal window next to the bed allows the owner to check the weather just by turning her head in the morning. The gem of the design, however, is the glass box inserted at ground level with milky glass plates. It stores garden and leisure goods and provides a translucent shrine for the automobile. From here you can explore the world—or escape from the floodwaters in style.

ARCHITECT:
Früh Architekturbüro, Hard (Austria)

LOCATION:
Hard (Austria)

COMPLETION:
2001

TYPE:
Showroom garage

VEHICLES:

Yellow awnings add to the house's sense of levity.

The basic design principle is particularly obvious when viewed from the garden.

Site plan

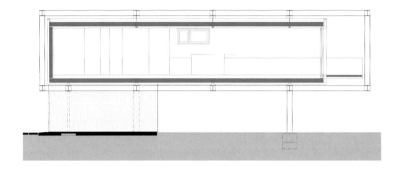

**Section
scale 1:200**

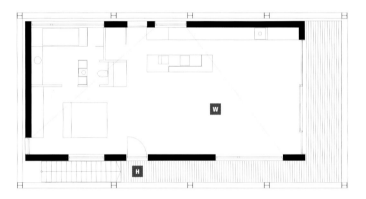

**Top floor
scale 1:200**

H entrance
W living area

**first floor
scale 1:200**

1 garage
2 driveway

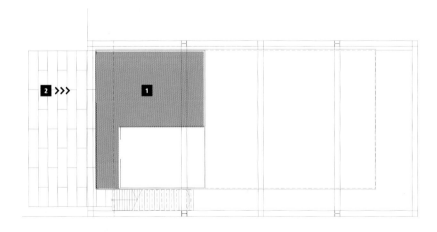

A translucent base houses the
garage and storage area.

ART HOUSE

Triath Gallery Multipurpose Building

ARCHITECT:
gerner°gerner plus,
Vienna (Austria)

LOCATION:
Grenzach-Wyhlen
(Germany)

COMPLETION:
2008

TYPE:
Showroom garage

VEHICLES:

In a low-density neighborhood of placid plaster-front houses, this owner wanted his art gallery to make a statement. The result is a two-story fair-faced concrete and glass structure that leans on a traditional gabled building on the west. On the opposite southeastern side, a long, open staircase sets the stage for the 20-meter-long (66-foot-long) gallery. Below is a glazed two-car garage on par with the exhibition space above. One hopes an upcoming show will feature vintage cars.

First floor
scale 1:200

1 garage
2 driveway
3 parking
H entrance

A transparent staircase leads to the exhibition level.

The first floor's glass display case makes a showroom of the garage.

LIVING IN COLOR

Amalia House

Covered in shocking green synthetic turf, Amalia House sits at the edge of a field in a small village in Styria. From a distance it disappears into the countryside, but up close it looks like a gigantic, casually placed toy, and its skin is fun to touch. This is a material one might put on a balcony, but who would make a building as capricious as this? Actually, the award-winning home is made from energy-saving, pre-fabricated wood modules; it has some 68 square meters (223 square feet) of living space and room for six beds. Opposing windows and doors allow one to see through the narrow, almost RV-like house, and they establish a playful connection between the landscape and houses's outer skin. The compact living-room bumpout features built-in furniture and outdoor overflow space to the left and right. Up a circular staircase, the second floor slides in the opposite direction. This move allowed for a step-out grass terrace over the living room, and at the other end, a cantilivered edge that provides dry parking below—that is, until the kids claim the space.

ARCHITECT:
GRID Architektur, Vienna (Austria)

LOCATION:
Kirchbach (Austria)

COMPLETION:
2007

TYPE:
Parking under the building

VEHICLE:

This unconventional house looks different from each vantage point.

Terraces flank the narrow living room.

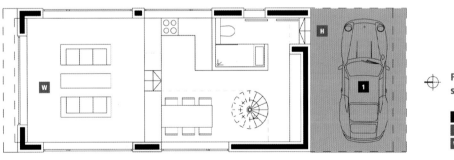

First floor scale 1:125

1 parking
H entrance
W living

The vacation home blends into the surrounding cornfields.

GARAGE WITH A DECK

W House

ARCHITECT:
heilergeiger architekten,
Kempten (Germany)

LOCATION:
Kempten (Germany)

COMPLETION:
2010

TYPE:
Garage box

VEHICLES:

Gone are the days when the color gray stood for buildings distant to human needs. Today fair-faced concrete is seen as a versatile building material that marries technology with the natural landscape from which it comes. That versatility includes its casting possibilities and the capacity to store heat and release it slowly. Heilergeiger Architeckten took avantage of those qualities in the design of this home, whose volumes are cleverly distributed on a narrow lot. The first floor contains a kitchen, dining room, and master bedroom, and at its center, a sculptural white staircase. The kitchen opens to a wind-protected patio, the result of a decision to pull the double garage to the front of the lot and add a connecting wall and second-story gangway. The garage's flat concrete roof was water-proofed and covered with larch decking, a move that expands the upstairs living space through sliding glass doors. A local metal workshop fabricated the steel garage door.

A small bridge connects the living room to a deck atop the garage.

The garage wall lends privacy and protection from the wind.

The garage roof becomes a lookout with a sweeping view of the neighborhood.

The cantilivered top floor
expands the children's rooms.

The patio extends the dining
room outdoors.

**Top floor
scale 1:200**

K children's
room
W living

**First floor
scale 1:200**

1 garage
2 driveway
H entrance

HIDING IN PLAIN SIGHT

F House

Formal innovation is not often found in the German single-family home. Comparatively high prices, limited lot sizes, and strict building codes result in practical solutions that rarely depart from the classic template. One exception is House F, designed by HPA+ Architektur in a neighborhood near the foothills of the Bergisches Land National Park. Its strict geometries and minimalist contours set it apart from other homes in the neighborhood. Windows were strategically placed to let in desired views and edit out others, and a distinctive bar of two-story glazing sweeps light into the central gallery, linking the open living quarters with the bedrooms upstairs. The 195-square-meter (640-square-foot) house has a geothermal heating and cooling system. Cars are discreetly housed in a two-garage car, a simple flat-roofed box wrapped in fiber-cement panels that suggest its functional independence. Seamlessly clad in the same material, the garage door is barely noticeable and startles passerby when it opens. The interlock between the garage and the house is particularly clever. The house is carved away, allowing the dark garage volume to push into its space, and creating a covered passageway to the front door.

ARCHITECT:
HPA+ Architektur,
Cologne (Germany)

LOCATION:
Bergisch Gladbach
(Germany)

COMPLETION:
2008

TYPE:
Lateral garage

VEHICLES:

The house's design language acknowledges neighborhood precedents while asserting its individuality.

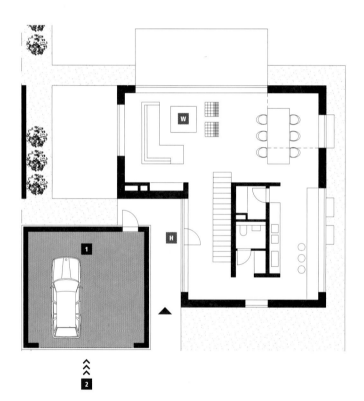

**First floor
scale 1:200**

1 garage
2 driveway
H entrance
W living

Site plan

The garage wall forms an edge to a small patio.

OPEN HOUSE

Water Pavilion

ARCHITECT:
Ian Shaw Architekten
BDA, Frankfurt at the
Main (Germany)

LOCATION:
Siegen (Germany)

COMPLETION:
2007

TYPE:
Integrated garage

VEHICLES:

A pavilion is an exciting project type, as its limited program and manageable size allow architects to blend conceptual and aesthetic qualities with rare clarity. The Manchester-born Frankfurt architect Ian Shaw took advantage of this opportunity to design a small lakefront building in Siegen. With the support of the discerning client, he created a modernist structure that cantilevers over the water—the perfect fishing platform. The framework of two horizontal 12 x

12-meter (39 x 39-foot) fair-faced concrete slabs sandwiches a 9 x 9-meter (30 x 30-foot) inner box and a glass-enclosed viewing area. The building also houses a three-car garage with 3 x 3-meter (10 x 10-foot) gates made of dark painted steel. As each one weighs some 340 kilograms (750 pounds), the client developed a ball-bearing mechanism that opens the doors with the push of a button.

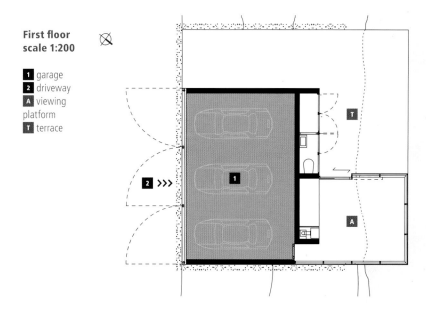

**First floor
scale 1:200**

1 garage
2 driveway
A viewing platform
T terrace

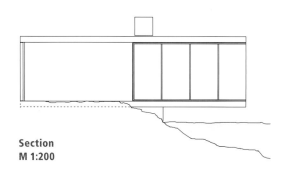

**Section
M 1:200**

In addition to its viewing platform, the pavilion houses three heavy garage bays that open with the touch of a button.

ONE FOR THE ROAD

R House

"It appears that having a preference for collecting bugs is a sign of success in life." This Charles Darwin quote could apply to car collections, too, which may be not only about success but the pure joy of living. The building is laid out as two volumes on the narrow lot, with the basement garage forming a connector beneath them. To the west is the office, while a two-story volume on the east contains the living spaces. These two volumes face each other across a terrace, and electronically activated glass doors provide the visual connection. The purpose of this trick is to stage the car collection, which ranges from everyday-use models to sports cars racing in international competitions such as the Mille Miglia. The climatized museum floor features a trophy corner and a workshop area with a service lift, dark parquet floor, and concrete walls inset with colorful car body panels. To get to the basement, each car passes through the office, where it is lowered on a scissor lift. This also allows the owner to float a car at whim, placing it next to the desk where it also can be admired from the house and terrace. Outside, a gabion wall and tree imagery imprinted on the home's facade reflect the surrounding landscape, as if the architect were conjuring a German country road.

ARCHITECT:
KÖGLARCHITEKTEN,
Fischach (Germany)

LOCATION:
close to Augsburg
(Germany)

COMPLETION:
2011

TYPE:
Underground garage

VEHICLES:

Living quarters occupy the rear
two-story section.

A car enthusiast's dream office: If necessary, one can read a book while sitting at the steering wheel.

The commodious garage
connects both building sections
underground and provides a
convenient place to park
multiple cars.

The living room looks across the terrace to the office, where cars are lowered into the basement garage on a platform.

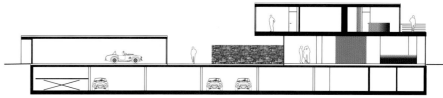

Section
scale 1:400

Lower level
scale 1:400

1 lift
2 garage
3 hydraulic ramp

First floor
scale 1:400

1 office
2 driveway
3 elevator
H entrance
W living

INSIDE OUT

K+H House

ARCHITECT:
Kunst+Herbert,
Hamburg (Germany)

LOCATION:
Hamburg (Germany)

COMPLETION:
2007

TYPE:
Integrated garage

VEHICLES:

**First floor
scale 1:200**

1 garage
2 driveway
H entrance
W living

Good architects distinguish themselves by solving even the thorniest spatial problems. Until recently, it was fairly unusual in Germany to see outdoor living spaces integrated into an urban plot. But as urban planners realize the need for denser cities, they are taking cues from Japan on how to make tight lots more livable. Hamburg architects Bettina Kunst and Christian Herbert based this design on the classic atrium house, which has proven its functionality over thousands of years. Originally a workshop had been built on the narrow parcel in a densely populated district of Hamburg, accessed as usual via the driveway to the main house.

The first step was to create an inner patio by opening up the flat roof and group the living areas in a U shape around it. Sliding glass doors link the bedroom, living room, and two offices to the interior courtyard, while skylights in the kitchen and bath let even more light into the 158-square-meter home (518-square-foot). A window above the kitchen sink, located in the rear of the house, opens up a sightline through the garage to the street. These moves make the house seem bigger than it is by carving out views to both public and private realms.

The garage can be seen from the kitchen. When the gate is open, the street is visible, too.

With rooms arranged in a U-shape around it, the interior courtyard expands the house's sense of space.

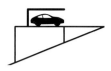

TOP JOB

Meier/Olave Home

ARCHITECT:
Marein Gijzen and
Daniel Gut, Zurich
(Switzerland)

LOCATION:
Ennetbaden (Switzerland)

COMPLETION:
2004

TYPE:
Parking on the roof

VEHICLES:

In plan, the small residence on the steep hill looks like the letter J. Living spaces occupy the two-story wing parallel to the valley—living, dining room, and kitchen above, bedrooms and baths below. The other service wing supports a carport on its roof, which is on grade with the driveway. Supported on slim diagonal braces, the pavilion-like enclosure's dark metal roof appears to float over the house, and its "walls" resemble a wire basket turned upside down. The glass entryway contributes to the building's visual lightness, illuminates the staircase, and artfully connects the architecture and landscape. One advantage of the house-car configuration is the protected inner patio formed by the building's two volumes. Set into the hillside, the concrete-block house, irregular stone-slab patio, and weightless car pavilion create an appealing material and spatial juxtaposition.

A glass-enclosed stairwell links the carport and main floor, contributing to the structure's sense of weightlessness.

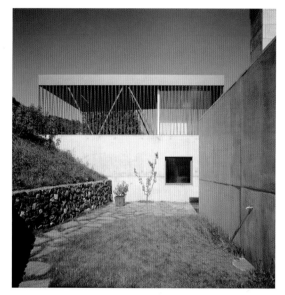

Shifting the house forward toward the valley expanded the rear garden.

The carport is on grade with the driveway and appears to float atop the concrete house.

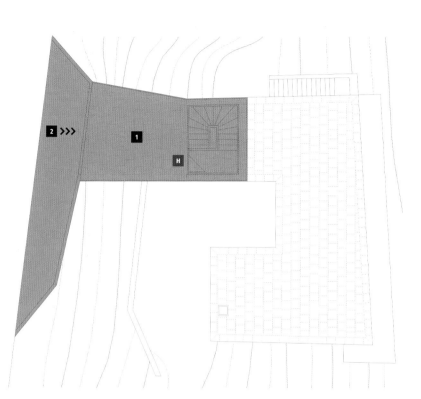

Site plan

First floor
scale 1:200

1 parking
2 driveway
H entrance

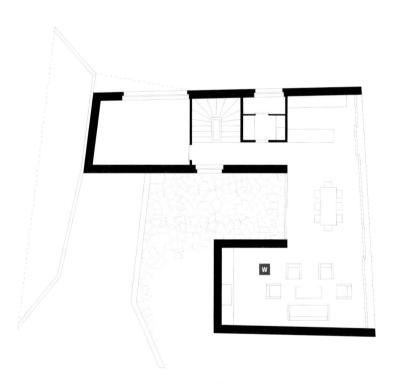

Lower floor
scale 1:200

W living

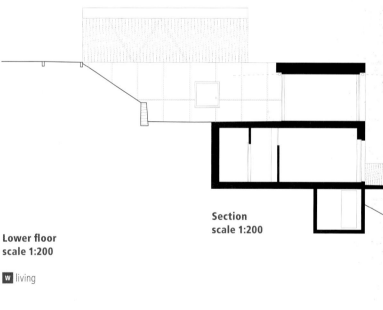

Section
scale 1:200

The house's J shape shelters an
interior patio.

ALPINE DREAMING

47°40'28''N/13°8'12''E House

You have to see this house to believe it. Consisting of two parallel steel-and-concrete slabs, it appears to float in a rural pasture, provocatively celebrating horizontality in an alpine panorama. The entire home resembles an exhibition pavilion. Apparently an ideal design match has occurred: clients who are extremely open-minded and an architectural studio with a strong vision. Nothing here is ordinary. Life inside the house is lived as if it were an enormous 500-square-meter (1,640-square-foot) stage, and the polished poured asphalt joins outdoor terraces and living spaces. Transparent walls underscore the interplay between inside and out. A woven polyethylene curtain can be closed to separate the terrace platform and its intermediate zone, which contains a swimming pool channel and an atrium for plants. The interior flows around nine wood modules finished in a screen-printed forest motif; they contain the storage, kitchen, and bathrooms. The main and guest sleeping areas can be divided with additional curtains. According to the architects, "the street starts inside the house," with two glassy garage bays on a platform. Four parking spaces are accessed through tilting, opaque polycarbonate panels, and stainless steel gullies drain water and snow slush.

ARCHITECT:
Maria Flöckner
and Hermann Schnöll
Salzburg (Austria)

LOCATION:
Adnet (Austria)

COMPLETION:
2007

TYPE:
Integrated showroom
garage

VEHICLES:

An exterior curtain communicates the unconventional concept at first glance.

View from the kitchen toward
the polycarbonate garage
doors..

Site plan

Dark freestanding
modules the roof.

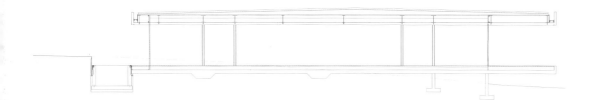

**Section
scale 1:250**

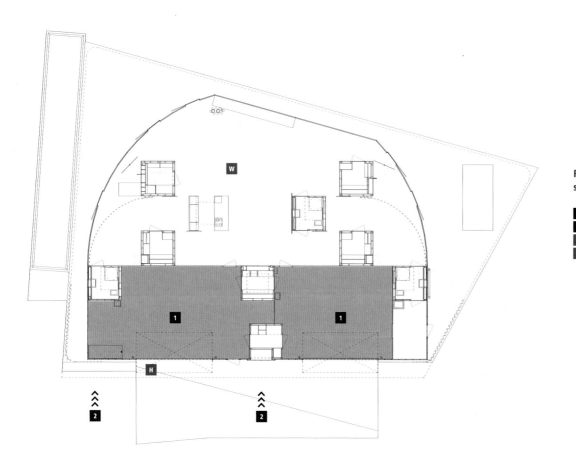

**First floor
scale 1:250**

1 garage
2 driveway
H entrance
W living

Gutters in the
garage floor shed
water and slush.

TUCKED UNDER

B in K House

ARCHITECT:
Matthias R Schmalohr,
Bückeburg (Germany)

LOCATION:
Krainhagen (Germany)

COMPLETION:
2007

TYPE:
Parking under the
building

VEHICLES:

Guests appreciate the obvious
main entryway: carport, door,
bell, and mailbox.

House B is a textbook example of the architect's capacity to respond to the ever-present constraints of restrictive building codes and uninspired surroundings. The gabled house reads as a simple black box with walls and roof wrapped entirely in fiber-cement slabs. Large windows and skylights brighten the interior's two-story volume and bamboo floors, and custom-made partitions slide into the wall, expanding the space where needed. The massive ground floor demonstrates its structural heft with the top floor visibly sitting on it and cantilevered towards the garden. A warmly colored bamboo staircase leads down to the entryway, where a large window turns the lounge area into a glazed transition zone between inside and outside. It also provides a view of the family car, which sits nice and dry under the protective box of the building.

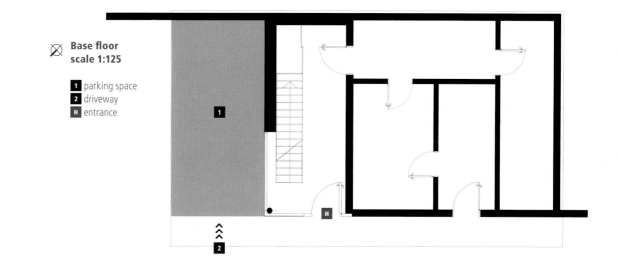

⊗ **Base floor
scale 1:125**

1 parking space
2 driveway
H entrance

Site plan

The occupants appreciate the
dry parking space with a direct
connection to the house.

NEXT STOP: LIVING ROOM

KRE House

ARCHITECT:
no. 555 – Takuya
Tsuchida, Yokohama
(Japan)

LOCATION:
Tokyo (Japan)

COMPLETION:
2008

TYPE:
Showroom garage

VEHICLES:

The client requested several unusual features for his home in an upscale neighborhood: a garage for nine vehicles—his favorite one inside the living room—and a tall tree. The entire structure had to be fitted onto a 200-square-meter (656-square-foot) lot, typical for Tokyo. In response, the architect came up with a one-story garage and large opening on the street, with a two-story tower recessed behind it. Open public spaces extend onto part of the garage roof, where the tree and the raised Lamborghini reside. Takuya Tsuchida enclosed the bedrooms, bathroom, playroom, and storage in lightweight steel boxes and hung them from the ceiling. Glass galleries provide views through the house. Once the beloved vehicle has been lowered and "put to bed" in the garage, the wood flooring lines up perfectly.

The vehicles are tightly parked on a red garage floor.

An elevator lifts the vehicle into the living area.

When the inconspicuous garage gate is lifted, the lavish interior is revealed.

**Section
without scale**

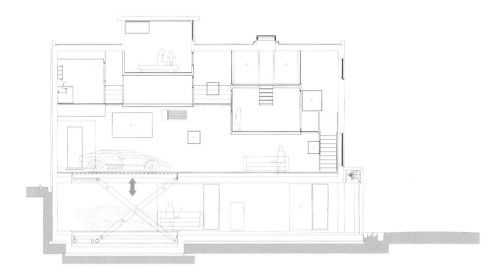

2

**First floor
scale 1:150**

1 garage
2 driveway
3 car lift
H entrance

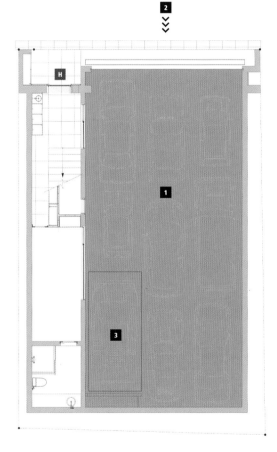

The nondescript garage box belies its interior tricks.

Once the floor is closed again the car becomes another piece of furniture. Suspended white boxes contain living spaces.

TILTED

Maison Zufferey

Imagine a relaxed drive on country roads that lead through a wine-growing region in the Swiss Rhône valley. A craggy rock wall rises dramatically over the scenery, preparing the traveler for an extraordinary sight. Nunatak Architectes Sarl, in Fully, a small town in the French-speaking Valais, referenced the Hausberg Mountain's extravagant tilt in one of its single-family homes in Leytron. The monolithic building, covered with slate slabs, appears to have fallen from the sky and hit the ground, becoming stuck at an angle. Only the windows are evidence of a livable interior with wood ceilings and white walls. Visitors are greeted at the entrance, where the west side of the building tilts up to expose its yellow-green underbelly, reflecting the color of its surroundings. A small floating metal staircase leads to an interior hallway. It is almost impossible to park more conveniently—protected from the sun and rain, with enough space to get in and out, and to load and unload.

ARCHITECT:
Nunatak Architectes Sarl, Fully (Switzerland)

LOCATION:
Leytron (Switzerland)

COMPLETION:
2003

TYPE:
Parking under the building

VEHICLES:

The house protrudes from the green valley floor as if it had fallen from the sky.

Maneuvering is easy on the generous parking surface.

A small steel staircase makes getting into the vehicle a conscious experience and divides the architecture from the landscape.

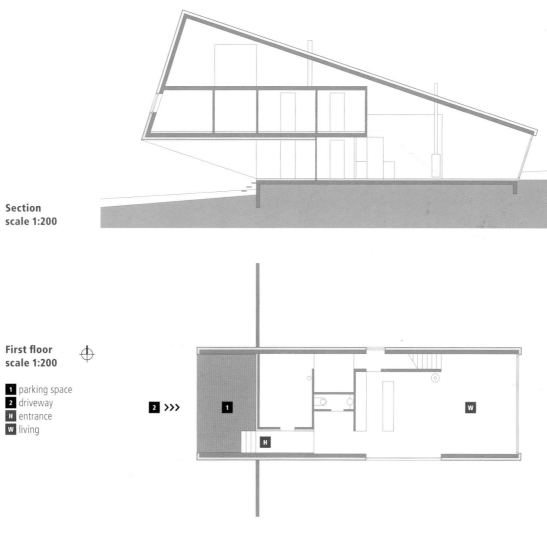

Section
scale 1:200

First floor
scale 1:200

1 parking space
2 driveway
H entrance
W living

The slanted building echoes the outline of the Hausberg Mountain. Only the windows indicate that the interiors are plumb.

TIN LANTERN

Grangegorman Residence

ARCHITECT:
ODOS Architects,
Dublin (Ireland)

LOCATION:
Dublin (Ireland)

COMPLETION:
2008

TYPE:
Integrated garage

VEHICLES:
🏍️ 🏍️ 🏍️

Garages aren't just for four-wheeled vehicles. This central Dublin townhouse's narrow entry gate offers a clue that the owner is a motorcycle enthusiast. The minimalist, shuttered building speaks the language of technology with its satin-finished aluminum panels, in contrast to the neighboring clinker brick facades and pointy gables. Nevertheless, the ground-level floor is based on traditional design: an open gate, garage workshop, and walled backyard, and the link between house and street is characteristic of an urban setting where neighbors stop by for a chat and cup of coffee. The 150-square-meter (492-square-foot) house's light-filled interior is reached via a steep staircase. A bedroom and bath occupy the first floor, while the top level houses a continuous living space visually enlarged with an integrated roof terrace. A screen of vertical aluminum blades provides privacy. Its semi-transparent surface contributes to the townhouse's elegantly proportioned facade.

The home's unmistakeable techno touch confronts tradition.

The garden wall's narrow opening makes clear that the garage is for bikes only.

**Section
scale 1:200**

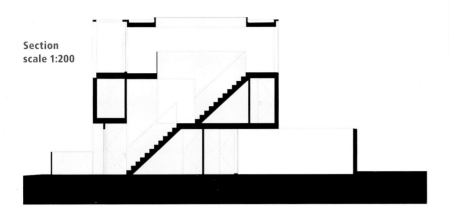

**First floor
scale 1:200** ⊗

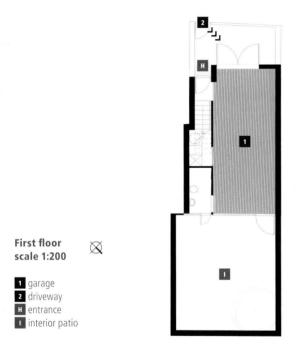

1 garage
2 driveway
H entrance
I interior patio

A skylight and shelving animate the entry hall and steep staircase typical of narrow townhouses.

The bike garage connects the streetfront to the rear inner patio.

LIGHT BOXES

House in Saijo

The small, meticulously finished home of Tokyo architect Kazuyuki Okumura stretches along a view of the Ishizuchi Mountain. Its neighbors embody the regional vernacular of tiled roofs and diminutive gardens. Okumura, however, based his concept on functional logic. The parcel's northern third is dedicated to mobility and contains a generous driveway and triple carport. Living quarters follow, organized in functional boxes reminiscent of tea pavilions, with three interior patios between them. The living area and kitchen open toward the garden on the south. Sliding doors on each module cool the house passively, and a small roof, accessed from a two-level "light tower," offers mountain views. On the hangar-like carport, a white double T-girder frame supports a skin of corrugated sheet metal, a nod to the parked cars. By contrast, the wood-clad bedroom cube behind it suggests domestic warmth and comfort.

ARCHITECT:
Kazuyuki Okumura, Tokyo (Japan)

LOCATION:
Saijo, Ehime (Japan)

COMPLETION:
2010

TYPE:
Carport

VEHICLES:

The home's modularity becomes clear when viewed from above. Public functions are in front, private spaces in back.

**First floor
scale 1:250**

1 parking space
2 driveway
H entrance
W living

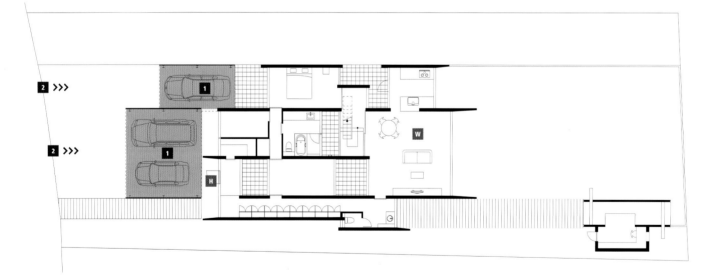

Inner windows and small atriums lend light and rhythm.

MATCHED BOOKENDS

Home in the Bergische Land

This contemporary home references the longhouse, originally built by Germanic settlers in the Bergische Land. A property's functions were combined under one long roof; living quarters were oriented toward the sun and view, while the stable occupied the other end of the building. Designed as an extruded tube, the 23-meter-long (75-foot-long) single-family home is clad in large fiber-cement panels, while warm Siberian larch boards line the recessed openings at each end. Taking advantage of the slope, the architects created an upper level containing the living areas and a balcony, and lower-level bedrooms spilling out to a terrace. The protected parking area reads as a gracious entry to the wheelchair-accessible house.

ARCHITECT:
oxen + partner architekten,
Hürth-Efferen (Germany)

LOCATION:
Rösrath (Germany)

COMPLETION:
2010

TYPE:
Carport

VEHICLES:

The longhouse's structural logic is immediately obvious.

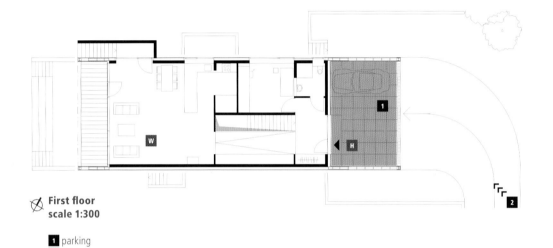

First floor
scale 1:300

1 parking
2 driveway
H entrance
W living

Section
scale 1:300

Site plan

Warm Siberian larch boards at each end of the house complement the smooth fiber-cement siding.

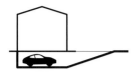

FIVE SQUARED

Basement Garage Under the Meadow

ARCHITECT:
Peter Kunz Architektur,
Winterthur (Switzerland)

LOCATION:
Herdern
at Winterthur (Switzer-
land)

COMPLETION:
1999

TYPE:
Underground garage

VEHICLES:
🚗🚗🚗🚗
🚗🚗🚗🚗

Only five gray squares are visible from atop a small hill in a flowering village pasture south of Lake Constance. Yet even at eye level these small gems retain their simplicity. The squares now turn into concrete cubes tucked into the natural slope, and a glass panel reveals a car parked in each. The client asked for a large garage that would fit inconspicuously into the landscape and provide a discriminating place for his cars. Winterthur architect Peter Kunz's response was an underground garage that elevates the demands of functional architecture and its need to retreat visually. His purist design concept combines sculptural formal language with the expressive qualities of a "secret." The cubes almost suck in the daylight and exhibit an interior world one is eager to explore. Such an enticing room becomes the perfect art gallery, supported by precise execution and lighting design. The main benefactors, however, are the cars, which turn heads inside their cozy display cases.

The cars turn heads inside their cozy display cases.

Square concrete garage boxes emerge from the hillside overlooking rural Lake Constance.

The garage's proportions, materials, and fixtures measure up to gallery standards.

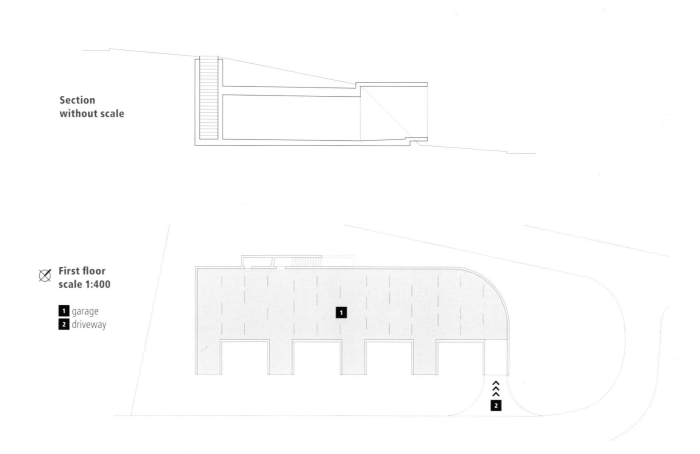

**Section
without scale**

⊗ **First floor
scale 1:400**

1 garage
2 driveway

Some of the most impressive
architectural concepts are those
that commune with nature.

ROUNDABOUT

O House

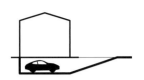

Perched on Lake Lucerne, this home's lot narrows by half at the waterfront. Yet there was still enough room to build a boathouse, small pier, and pool and spa. And it was precisely this irregular terrain that inspired the shape of the house, designed by Zurich-based architect Philippe Stuebi. The client's wish for a roundabout driveway was another dominant factor in its design. A round skylight set into the circular driveway lights the underground garage—a geometric motif that carries through on the concrete facade. While the exterior evokes free-wheeling 1970s aesthetic, the interior is a surprise, with a two-story orangery and exotic plants at the entrance. From here, visitors are ushered south to the kitchen, dining, and living areas and their panoramic lake views. An opening in the protruding loggia continues the circular motif, as does the terrace paving and light fixtures in the commodious garage, which holds at least 12 vehicles.

ARCHITECT:
Philippe Stuebi Architekten, Zurich (Switzerland) with Eberhard Tröger

LOCATION:
Lake Lucerne (Switzerland)

COMPLETION:
2007

TYPE:
Underground garage

VEHICLES:

The block-like house gives passersby a sneak peek of Lake Lucerne.

A world of cars only revealed to a few. The wheel motif is everywhere.

Curtain walls frame panoramic views of Lake Lucerne, including the boathouse roof visible in the background.

The pool connects interior and exterior. A staircase leads from the living room down to the lakeshore.

First floor
scale 1:400

1 parking
2 driveway
H entrance
W living

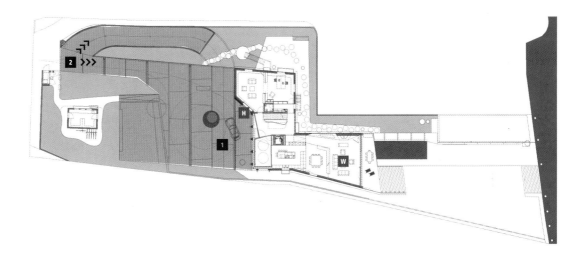

Lower level
scale 1:400

1 garage
2 driveway

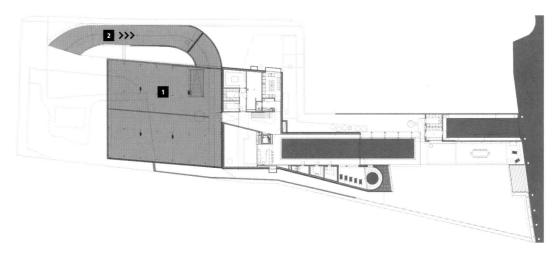

Strong visual motifs have a memorable effect.

POWER PARKING

Villa 1

ARCHITECT:
Powerhouse Company,
Rotterdam (Netherlands)

LOCATION:
Arnhem (Netherlands)

COMPLETION:
2008

TYPE:
Integrated garage

VEHICLES:

One would have to walk the whole way around this futuristic-looking house to identify its Y-shaped floor plan—and a circular path through the pine forest invites that journey. Every functional aspect was given a distinctive design and detailing. The long wing's lower floor houses two guest rooms, a bathroom, and a joint patio; the short wing contains the main bedroom. A garage is at the center, accessed by way of a ramp from the sinuous driveway. Only exceptional vehicles would look at home within its semi-circular walls made from folded stainless steel. The transparent top floor extends centrifugally in three directions. It contains a large hall with a fireplace and areas dedicated to multimedia, music, and books. The short section contains the kitchen, which retreats inconspicuously behind one of the three modular furniture-like pieces. The curved module on the north side is lined with American walnut and contains an integrated staircase, bathroom, and guest room. Another module wrapped in Norwegian slate houses the kitchen, storage, a bathroom, and a bar. A third module, made of concrete, contains the fireplace, shelves, and a projector.

A pathway circles the house, the better to view it from all directions.

The shimmering white house lies flat on the forest floor, with the garage tucked beneath.

The entrance module hides a staircase.

Site plan

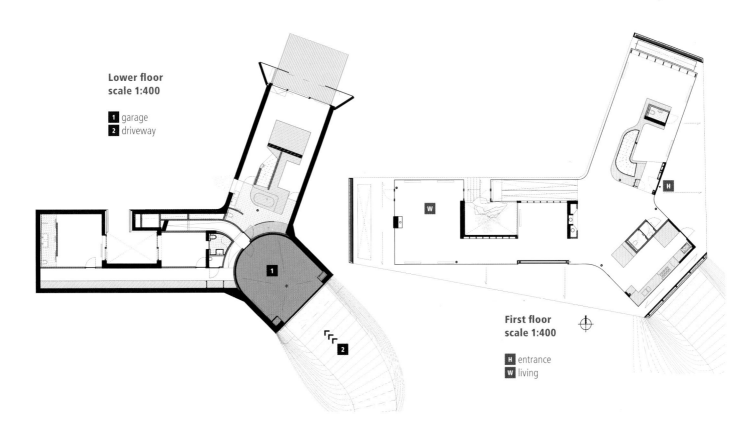

**Lower floor
scale 1:400**

1 garage
2 driveway

**First floor
scale 1:400**

H entrance
W living

Even a subterranean garage can
look polished.

RESIDENCE WITH A RUNWAY

Aatrial House

ARCHITECT:
Robert Konieczny –
KWK Promes, Katowice
(Poland)

LOCATION:
Opole (Poland)

COMPLETION:
2006

TYPE:
Integrated garage

VEHICLES:

KWK Promes is one of the most innovative architecture firms in Poland, as evidenced by its Aatrial house. It's hard to believe that this is a single-family home and not something else—a museum, for example. The 660-square-meter (2,165-square-foot) concrete-and-steel box hovers over a rough granite base, commanding its structural elements with the ambition of a James Bond home. A cobblestone ramp stops in front of two silver garage doors, and you can almost hear the eight-cylinder engine cutting off while the automatic gate closes silently behind it. Owners enter through the service area next to the garage, or through the front door—a glass slab that pushes obliquely into the atrium. Two bedrooms occupy the upper floors, each with a terrace from which to enjoy the garden and open landscape beyond.

Cars enter the atrium where two gates open automatically.

Pedestrians enter on a stone staircase.

The unreality of the photo is intended. It shows that even extraordinary requests can be realized.

First floor
scale 1:300

1 garage
2 driveway
H entrance
W living

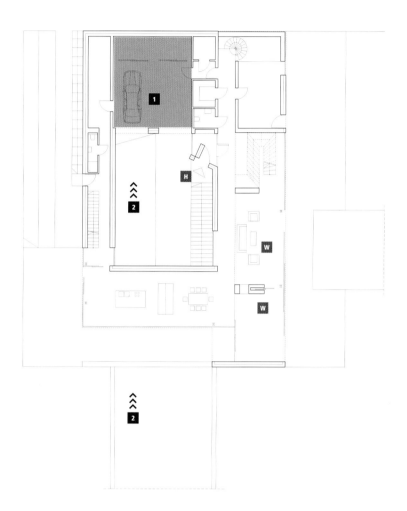

The interior design incorporates generous lighting and an open layout. The two-floor living room hall is located on the garden side of the building.

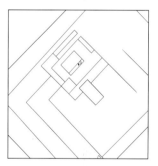

Site plan

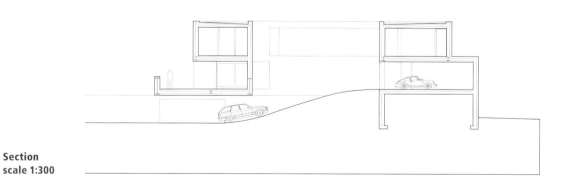

Section
scale 1:300

The runway and underpass tell drivers in no uncertain terms that they have arrived.

AUTUMN SYMPHONY

Furniture House No. 5

Designed by well-known Japanese architect Shigeru Ban and his U.S. colleague Dean Maltz, this home sits in an upscale vacation home community in the Hamptons. A series of pillar-like cabinet modules made from untreated wood support the enormous roof plate, while providing ample storage and housing the mechanical equipment. Like a Japanese country home with its centrifugal wings, this "furniture house" is arranged in sections, with the cabinet blocks providing screen-like walls. The cabinetry begins at the wonderfully light carport, defines the arrival sequence, and screens the vehicles from the house. Glass walls put the natural environment on constant display. The L-shaped rear wing contains four bedrooms and baths and forms an edge to the pool terrace, which has a built-in grill. On summer days, family life shifts outside to enjoy the water, landscape, and architecture.

ARCHITECT:
Shigeru Ban / Dean Maltz, New York (USA)

LOCATION:
Sagaponac, Long Island, N.Y. (USA)

COMPLETION:
2006

TYPE:
Carport

VEHICLES:

Structural V-braces echo those on the carport.

This vacation home invites the landscape inside.

**Sections
without scale**

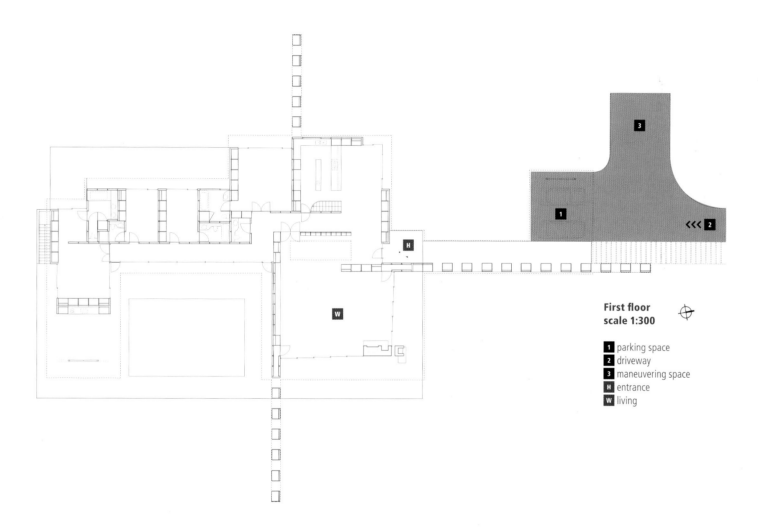

Site plan

**First floor
scale 1:300**

1	parking space
2	driveway
3	maneuvering space
H	entrance
W	living

The vacation home
opens into the
landscape. Cabinet
modules continue into
the garden.

TYROLEAN NOBLESSE

House PM

ARCHITECT:
S.O.F.A. Architekten,
Vienna (Austria)

LOCATION:
Meran (Italy)

COMPLETION:
2007

TYPE:
Integrated garage
and parking space

VEHICLES:

Building on a hillside can be daunting, but here the architects used the terrain to their advantage. They set the home into the slope like a dam and placed the kitchen, living room, and guest quarters on the ground-level floor, which is served by a wooden terrace. The middle floor, set toward the rear garden, contains a large reception area, library, and office, and shades the lower floor and terrace. Upstairs, two bedroom blocks occupy the front and side. The main bedroom protrudes over the entrance, creating a covered space that serves as a carport and complementing a double garage at the rear that provides additional storage. Cladding the exterior are 12-mm-thick (.5-inch-thick) glass fiber-reinforced concrete panels that add to the sense of mass, particularly at the entrance areas, where the garage gate and entry door almost disappear. Beneath the overhangs, light-colored panels and perimeter light strips illuminate the spaces below.

A covered area at the house's entrance offers an additional carport illumuniated by commercial light strips.

Lawn, wooden deck, or roof terrace —any of these outdoor destinations feature a fantastic landscape view.

Site plan

The open-tread staircase and cleverly articulated volumes admit light and views.

A glass slot cut into the slanted roof funnels light to the lower level.

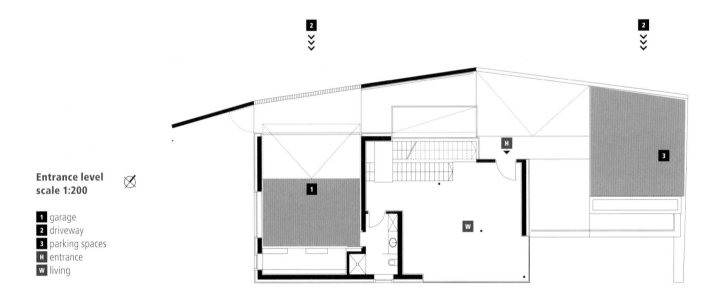

**Entrance level
scale 1:200**

1 garage
2 driveway
3 parking spaces
H entrance
W living

The garage door fits seamlessly
into the homogenous facade.

SOUTERRAIN GALLERY

Glass Pavilion

ARCHITECT:
Steve Hermann Design
& Development,
Montecito (USA)

LOCATION:
Montecito (USA)

COMPLETION:
2010

TYPE:
Integrated showroom
garage

VEHICLES:

The "exhibit hall" looks out on
the park-like garden.

Architects often have difficulty designing their own homes, as they are too close to the project to be objective. And so it took Steve Hermann six years to develop this large, 1,290-square-meter (4,232-square-foot) villa on a densely vegetated lot. Passing through a transparent glass gate, visitors follow a stone slab pathway that curves across the lawn to the house. From this perspective, the building resembles a weightless, U-shaped double slab resting on the ground. This effect is further enhanced by spotlights affixed to the overhangs and by offset pathway slabs piling up to form the entrance staircase. Full-height windows visually merge the modernist interior and idyllic garden. The

floor plan is spatially luxurious, from the unstructured living area to the master bedroom and a huge bathroom with a dressing room—which can be viewed from all sides or closed off with a screen. The rear section is more opaque and incorporates a full lower level. Here, a long terrace with loungers invites sunbathing, and a glass wall reveals the interior's art gallery and car collection. (The cars arrive via a driveway ramp that cuts under the front of the house). Positioning the vehicles on the shiny floor is no problem, as there is ample space for maneuvering. If you want to view them behind glass, splendidly spotlighted, all you need to do is turn your lounger around.

The house has become famous for its garage-cum-art gallery.

The office's ribbon
window frames a view to
the owner's prized cars.

The cars are showcased against a lush backdrop.

The showroom lies through the garage doors to the left, while everyday vehicles head to the right. Above is the master bath.

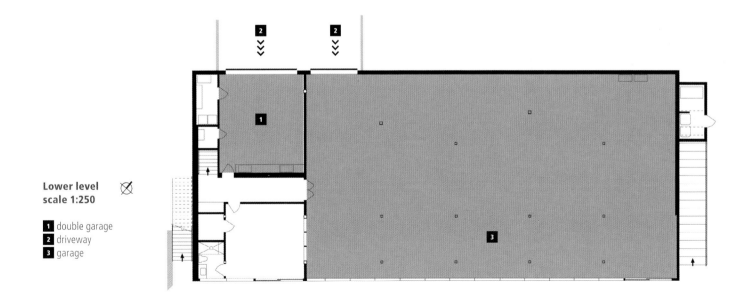

Lower level
scale 1:250

1 double garage
2 driveway
3 garage

CURVED COMFORT

Villa F

If you think of residential architecture as a brick box with a saddle roof, and if you are convinced that floors and walls must be straight, then you are bound to get a different view of things here in Franconia. The young Rothenburg-based Studio Martin Schroth placed a real gem of a villa among the stock of old trees in a tasteful neighborhood. Its rigorous design pushes the boundaries of conventionality, renouncing typical horizontal structuring to achieve a more dynamic living style. Ceilings slide into each other and expand the generous living areas. Continuous lateral glazing opens the villa towards the garden and pool, which is accessed by a staircase reminiscent of Mies van der Rohe's stair at Tugendhat house. A bright travertine terrace adds to the white building's elegance.

The split-level floor plan not only allows space to flow, it also separates the bedroom and living areas. While the bedrooms are located on the two top floors, the wellness area occupies the lowest level next to a garden. This is where the quadruple garage is located, its floor merging seamlessly with the driveway. The glass wall not only illuminates a typically dark parking zone, it also provides views out from the adjacent room.

ARCHITECT:
Studio Martin Schroth, Rothenburg on the Tauber (Germany)

LOCATION:
close to Neustadt at the Aisch (Germany)

COMPLETION:
2010

TYPE:
Integrated garage

VEHICLES:

The floors' gentle curves becomes the house's motif.

The entry gate's etched patterns foreshadow the home's unique features.

Full-height glass walls on the garden illuminate the leisure room and the generously sized garage.

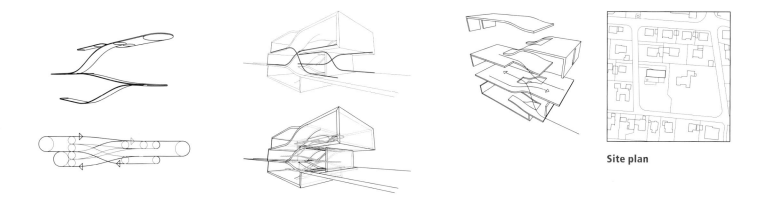

Site plan

Section
scale 1:200

House and car share some of
the same aerodynamics.

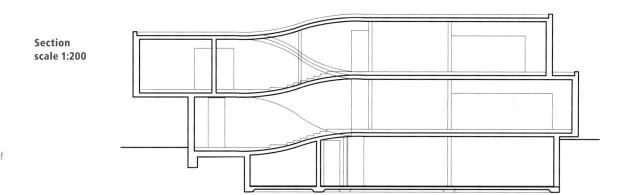

Lower level
scale 1:200

1 garage
2 driveway
H lower entrance
W wellness

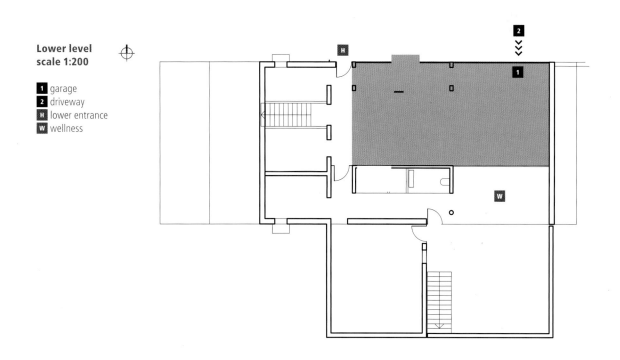

The floor gently rises in the
living area and incorporates a
comfortable sofa.

VIEWFINDER

House in Petersberg

This inscrutable 205-square-meter (673-square-foot) home sits on a downward–sloping lot in the east Hessian town of Petersberg. A slot in its monolithic street facade welcomes two cars while framing views of the valley below. The parking pad—the roof of a lower volume— offers plenty of space for unloading groceries and quickly stashing bicycles and umbrellas. Inside, the central entry level conveniently accommodates the home's utilitarian functions such as storage, laundry, and trash. The floor above contains kitchen, dining, and living areas, which benefit from a glassy rear facade and terrace running the length of the house. On the lower level, an integrated patio serves the main bathroom, bedrooms, and library. If required, the guest room can be retrofitted as a separate unit with its own entrance. Building materials echo the home's pure form: prefabricated concrete walls and stone and wood floors.

ARCHITECT:
Sturm and Wartzeck, Dipperz (Germany)

LOCATION:
Petersberg-Steinau (Germany)

COMPLETION:
2004

TYPE:
Carport

VEHICLES:

Although the front door is not visible, the strong street facade leaves no doubt as to its location.

View of the bedroom from the small loggia leading up to the utility room and the guest area.

The linear parking aperture under the house frames a dramatic view.

Site plan

First floor
scale 1:200

1 parking
2 driveway
H entrance

Top floor
scale 1:200

W living

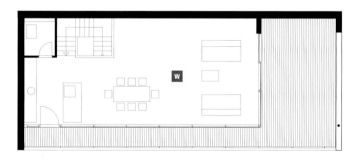

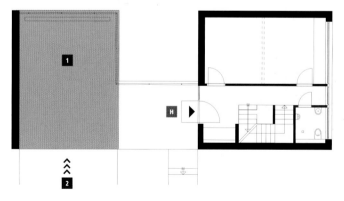

The valley side reveals the
upper floor's generous glass
walls and a roof terrace.

RURAL URBANITY

S/M/L House

A plan view reveals the organization of this development project, which sits on a square footprint. The design program included offices for a communications company, two living units, and space for a private car collection. Titus Bernhard Architekten addressed these requirements by designing three long, rectangular buildings that clearly signal to visitors the public and private areas. The base, cut into a gently sloping hillside, features paving materials that differentiate the spaces: stone slabs for the workplace vehicles, gravel for the semi-public residential area in front of the garage and the piazza between the buildings. A wooden terrace and pool face discreetly toward nature. The commercial building's steel-and-concrete skeleton and two-color coated glass create an appealing rhythm of openness and privacy. This interplay repeats itself on the more opaque two-level living units. The result is a cohesive compound with differentiated functions. The residential section's 40 x 27-meter (131 x 86-foot) fair-faced-concrete-clad ground floor accommodates basement rooms and a vintage car collection. With its opaque glass sliding doors, this collector's garage becomes a display case, particularly at night, and holds its own against the adjacent architecture.

ARCHITECT:
Titus Bernhard Architekten, Augsburg (Germany)

LOCATION:
Burgrieden
at Laupheim (Germany)

COMPLETION:
2002

TYPE:
Collector's garage

VEHICLES:

A small patio with almost rural appeal sits between the front office wing and two private homes at the rear.

The street facades glow at night.

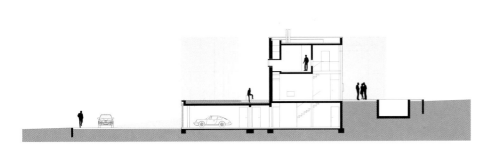

**Section
without scale**

Site plan

**Base level
scale 1:300**

1 garage
(collector's vehicles)
2 driveway
3 garage (vehicles
for daily use)

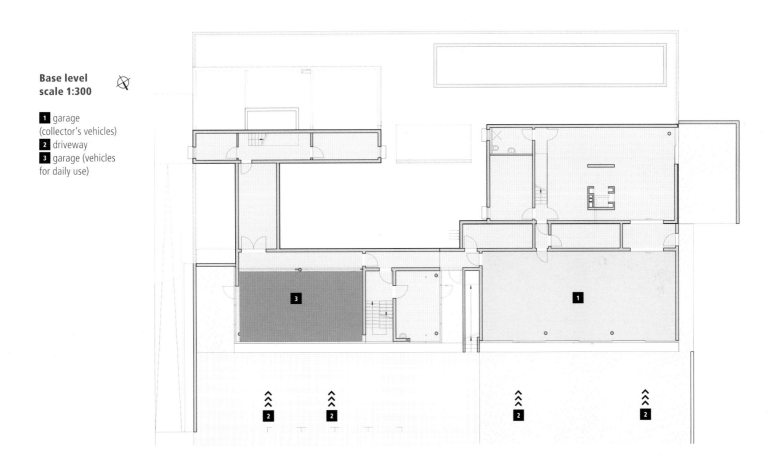

When the gates are open the
vintage treasures take center
stage. In fair weather they can
be parked on the gravel pad in
front of the building.

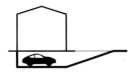

SUPERNATURAL UNDERWORLD

Villa at the Lake

ARCHITECT:
Unger & Treina AG,
Zurich (Switzerland)

LOCATION:
Lake Lucerne
(Switzerland)

COMPLETION:
2009

TYPE:
Collector's garage

VEHICLES:

A section view of this distinctive villa reveals an upper world and an underworld, and both realms are equally attractive. The sloping property is accessed from the street at the bottom of the lot, at a transparent entrance portal next to a huge house number. As if it were an arty mining tunnel, the 20-meter-long (67-foot-long) passage is encased in irregular fair-faced concrete blocks and leads to an elevator. Given the steep terrain, the elevator rises almost three levels until it reaches the lower floor of the three-story home. From this level, a sculptural staircase leads upwards, lighted by panoramic windows. The home's angular forms mirror the alpine peaks surrounding the house and Lake Lucerne. Take your pick of destinations: the living room overlooking the lake, the office facing the Bürgenstock Mountain peak, or the bedroom oriented toward Mount Rigi. The house also contains a spa area, outdoor pool, and theater, and its floors are made of oiled wenge wood and black basalt. A spacious underground garage holds a Porsche collection, displayed through a windowed entrance. The garage houses a showroom, lounge, workshop, lighting and sound systems, and even a car lift.

The vintage Porsches' streamlined contours create an interesting contrast with the house's nested cubes.

The villa's moodily lit entrance tunnel consists of irregularly placed fair-faced concrete walls. An elevator awaits at the end of the corridor.

As a prized car emerges, the reason for this elaborate, vault-like space becomes clear.

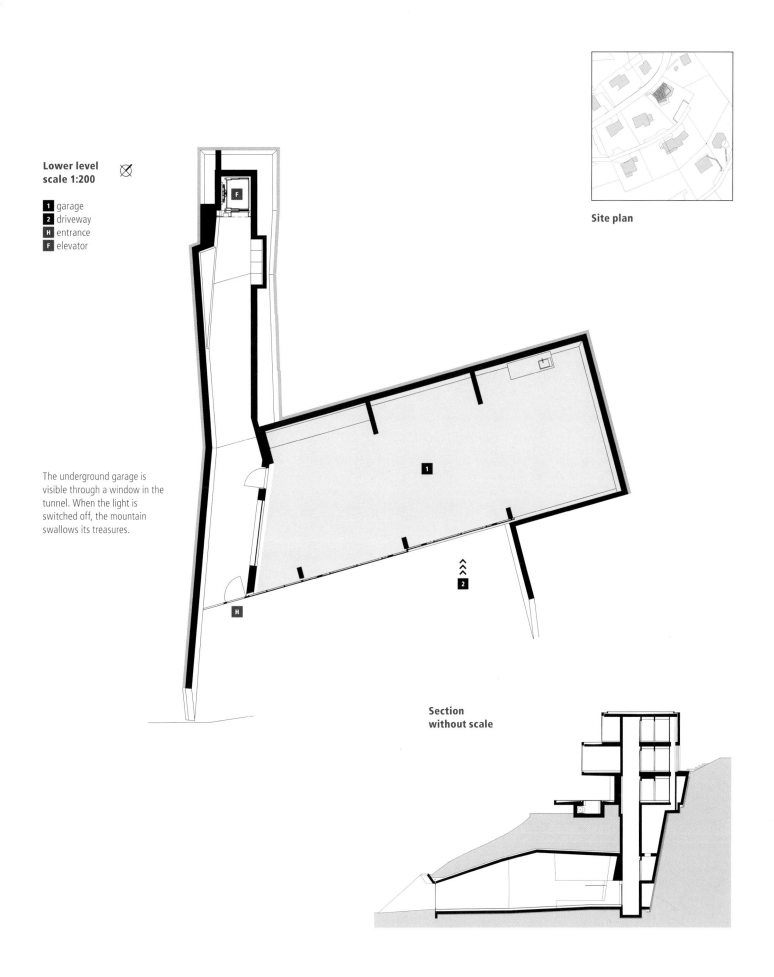

**Lower level
scale 1:200** ⊗

1 garage
2 driveway
H entrance
F elevator

The underground garage is
visible through a window in the
tunnel. When the light is
switched off, the mountain
swallows its treasures.

Site plan

**Section
without scale**

A sophisticated collector's
garage includes a workshop,
lounge area, and light and
sound installations.

FROM CONCEPT CAR TO ARCHITECTURAL CONCEPT

Jan R. Krause

They could not be more different: mobile and immobile, vehicle and architecture. Both are highly valued in our society and express our cultural and societal identity. The automobile takes us away, provides a sense of freedom, and fulfils its purpose through movement. Ultimately, however, a voyage is characterized by its points of departure and arrival, and hence by our built environment.

The architectural award "Better Parking" ("Schöner Parken") documents this relationship. The Italian sports car manufacturer Maserati and the German building manufacturer Eternit initiated the call for entries that featured special places for special automobiles. The architects of the jury, Barbara Holzer from Zurich, Astrid Bornheim from Berlin, and Gerhard Wittfeld from Aachen, recognized exceptional homes with strong design concepts, innovative use of materials, and particular attention to detail. Twelve of the forty houses in this book participated in the "Better Parking" competition.

They clearly show the interconnections between car and architecture. Even though the car is a mass-produced item while architecture is a singular occurrence expressing an individual cultural concept, both follow a similar design process. It starts with a rough sketch and continues with the development of model studies and detailed refinement, justifying the object's value for the future owner. In the end, both architecture and car manufacturing should result in a unique product that reflects the client's personal interpretation and individuality.

Both car production and architecture generate ideas that mature during the planning stage to find their final spatial expression. In the case of the automobile, prototypes and concept cars create this dialogue with the end user. Auto exhibitions are subjected to the votes of specialized media and visitors. While these concept cars usually do not reach the serial production stage, some have had a significant impact, such as the Maserati Boomerang, developed in 1971 by Italian designer Giorgetto Giugaro. The extreme wedge-shaped sports car, with its unadorned objectivity and knife-edge angles like folded paper, became influential during that decade. Giugiaro later incorporated some of those ideas into the first series of the VW Golf.

Concept houses, which have a wide influence, occur in architecture, too. One example is the experimental Case Study Houses designed by renowned architects such as Richard Neutra, Charles and Ray James, Pierre Koenig, and Eero Saarinen. Not all were built, but they played a significant role in the development of modern architecture.

Jan Krause is a professor for architecture and media management at Bochum College and leads the Eternit Akademie as well as the marketing and communications department of the Eternit AG company.

Architecture award "Better Parking": first place winners, page 98, Kunst+Herbert; page 128, Peter Kunz Architektur.

The "Better Parking" exhibition focused on the conceptual, with the Maserati Boomerang as the leitmotif. Three of that luxury car's characteristics found their way into the entry by Berlin architect Astrid Bornheim: a linear flow suggesting speed, the wire-frame model that is so important to the design process, and the vehicles' interior finishes. With the help of experimental model building, the Boomerang is rendered as an abstract vector graphic and cut into an Eternit wall of 50 square meters. A counter in front of it continues the motif as a cutout pattern. The image's 256 shades of gray were analyzed and divided into horizontal lines and then cut into a twelve-millimeter-thick Eternit plate with custom cutting software. The corresponding gray color gradient was calculated as a specific cutting depth. This results in surprising visual effects, with the raster image changing or dissolving, depending on the light and viewing angle.

Exhibition architecture reflects the connection between automobile design and architecture on a conceptual and experimental level and provides a behind-the-scenes look at the development process. Apart from the similarities of process and object, one distinct factor ultimately unites home and car: a passion for something special.

The experimental exhibition architecture of Astrid Bornheim for the "Better Parking" contest is based on the Boomerang, the legendary concept car by Maserati. Here it is cut into an Eternit wall as an abstract line graphic.

Jan R. Krause is professor for architecture and media management at Bochum College. Since 2003, he has taught a masters-level class on public relations for architects. Krause leads the Eternit Akademie and the marketing and company communications division of the Eternit AG company. After studying architecture in Braunschweig, Zurich, and Vienna, he studied public relations at the journalist academy of Baden-Wuerttemberg and was the editor of the architecture magazine AIT. He studied management strategy, finance, marketing, and human resources on a post-graduate level at the Vlerick Leuven Gent Management School in Belgium.

Krause is the author of the book *Architekturvermittlung (Architecture Agency)*. He writes for architecture and economics publications and is a member of the editorial staff of the architecture magazine *A+D Architektur und Detail*. Krause is a jury member of several architecture competitions and curator of architecture exhibitions. He has organized and hosted international architecture conferences, workshops, and seminars. From 2003 to 2009 he was on the board of the German Werkbund Berlin, including three years as its chairman. In 2007 he was appointed to the Konvent der Bundesstiftung für Baukultur. He lives in Berlin.

Prof. Dipl.-Ing. Jan R. Krause AMM | Architektur Media Management
Hochschule Bochum | Fachbereich Architektur
Lennershofstraße 140 | 44801 Bochum
jan.krause@hs-bochum.de | www.amm-bochum.de

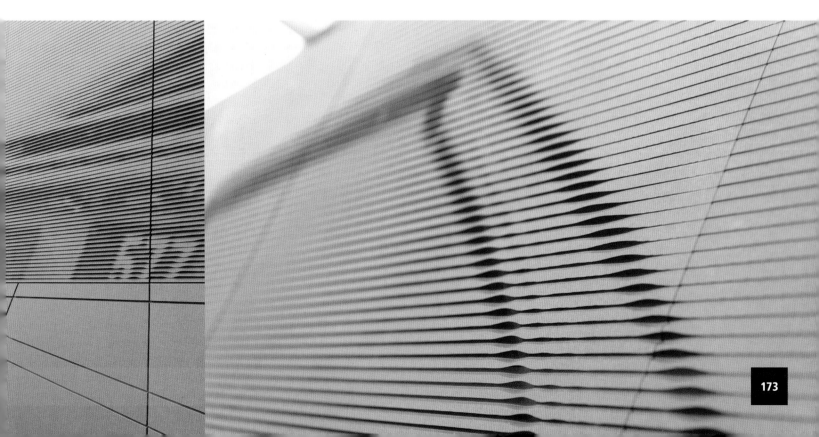

ARCHITECTS' REGISTER

03 Architekten GmbH
Andreas Garkisch, Karin Schmid,
Michael Wimmer
Architekten BDA, Stadtplaner
DASL
Hermann-Lingg-Straße 10
D-80336 Munich
www.03muenchen.de
photos: Simone Rosenberg /
Florian Holzherr (S. 33)

Andreas Fuhrimann,
Gabrielle Hächler
Architekten ETH BSA SIA AG
Hardturmstrasse 66
CH-8005 Zurich
www.afgh.ch
photos: Valentin Jeck

AFF Architekten
project leader: Robert Zeimer
Wedekindstraße 24
D-10243 Berlin
www.aff-architekten.com
photos: AFF Architekten

Architekturbüro Stocker
Uhlandstraße 1 a
D-72620 Remshalden
www.atelier-stocker.de
photos: Brigida Gonzáles

Astrid Bornheim Architek-
tur
Anklamer Straße 25
D-10115 Berlin
www.astridbornheim.de
photos: David Franck, Ostfildern

Atelier Tekuto Co. Ltd.
Projekt Architekten: Yasuhiro
Yamashita + Yoichi Tanaka
Yasuhiro Yamashita
Architecture Studio
4-1-20-B1F Jingumae,
Shibuya-ku, J-Tokio, 150-0001
www.tekuto.com / http://
tekuto2.squarespace.com/
photos: Makoto Yoshida / Jimmy
Cohrssen (page 47)

bonnard woeffray
Architectes Fas SIA
Clos-Donroux 1
CH-1870 Monthey
www.bwarch.ch
photos: Hannes Henz / Benjamin
Krampulz (page 50)

C18 Architekten
new company name:
kaestle ocker roeder Architekten
Hölderlinstraße 40
D-70193 Stuttgart
www.kaestleockerroeder.de
photos: Brigida Gonzáles

COAST OFFICE ARCHITEC-
TURE
Helfferichstraße 1
D-70192 Stuttgart
www.coastoffice.de
photos: David Franck / Valentin
Jeck (page 58 and 61)

CSD Architecten
Crepain, Spaens, Debie
Architecten
9, Vrijdagmarkt
B-2000 Antwerp
www.csdarchitecten.be
photos: Luc Roymans

Dongus Architekten
Seestraße 13
D-71229 Leonberg
www.dongus-architekten.de
photos: Christian Schaulin

drewes + strenge
architekten bda
Berlin/Herzebrock/San Francisco
Bahnhofstraße 10 a
D-33442 Herzebrock-Clarholz
photos: Christian Richters

Elke Reichel Architekten
GmbH
Bismarckstraße 63
D-70197 Stuttgart/Marienberg
www.elkereichel.com
photos: Johannes-Maria
Schlorke

Fran Silvestre Arquitectos
project architect: Fran Sylvestre,
Maria José Sáez
interior design: Alfaro Hofmann
project team: David Gallardo
Llopis, Carlos Garcia Mateo,
Pedro Vicente López López, José
Vicente Miguel López, José
Ángel Ruiz Millo, Fernando Usó
Martin, Alexandre Marcos, Jorge
Lucas Abad; assistant: Sara
Sancho Ferreras
San Vicente Martir 160, 1
E-46007 Valencia
www.fransilvestrearquitectos.
com
photos: Fernando Alda

Früh Architekturbüro ZT
GmbH
Lochbachstraße 6
A-6971 Hard
www.frueh.at
photos: Adi Bereuter

gerner°gerner plus
Andreas and Gerda Maria
Gerner
Mariahilfer Straße 101 / 3 / 49
A-1060 Vienna
www.gernergernerplus.com
photos: Manfred Seidl /
Didier Leroi (page 81)

GRID Architektur GmbH
Isabella Straus, Ric Thill,
Gerhard Klocker
Hammer-Purgstallgasse 5/4
A-1020 Vienna
www.grid-architektur.com
photos: Lukas Schaller /
Stuhlhofer/Wolf (page 85)

heilergeiger architekten
Fürstenstraße 42
D-87439 Kempten
www.heilergeiger.de
photos: Hermann Rupp

HPA$^+$ Architektur
Dipl.-Ing. Architekt Lars Puff
Dipl.-Ing. Architekt Dorothee
Vicario
Boisseréestraße 12
D-50674 Cologne
www.hpa.de
photos: Detlef Podehl

Ian Shaw Architekten BDA
RIBA
Helmholtzstraße 35
D-60385 Frankfurt at the Main
www.shaw-architekten.de
photos: Felix Krumbholz

KÖGLARCHITEKTEN
Blumenstraße 10
D-86850 Fischach
Tel.: 08236/96130
www.koeglarchitekten.de
photos: Weiss advertizing
photography

Kunst+Herbert
Christian Herbert, Bettina Kunst
Büro für Forschung und Hausbau
Henriettenweg 1
D-20259 Hamburg
www.kunstherbert.de
photos: Olaf Hauschulz / Oliver
Heissner (page 99)

Marein Gijzen and Daniel
Gut
Bürokontakt: Gut & Schoep
Architekten GmbH
Dipl.-Arch. ETH SIA
Quellenstrasse 27
CH-8005 Zurich
www.gutschoep.ch
photos: Roger Frei

Maria Flöckner
and Hermann Schnöll
architect DI Maria Flöckner
architect Mag. Arch. Hermann
Schnöll
Lasserstraße 6 a
A-5020 Salzburg
www.floecknerschnoell.com
photos: Stefan Zenzmaier /
Christoph Theurer (page 105)

Matthias R Schmalohr
Röcker Straße 5
D-31675 Bückeburg
www.schmalohr.net
photos: Klaus Dieter Weiss

no. 555
Architectural Design
Office
Takuya Tsuchida
5-223 Yamamoto-cho, Naka-ku,
Yokohama-shi, Kanagawa,
Japan
www.number555.com
photos: Koichi Torimuri /
Shunichi Koyama / Takuya
Tsuchida

Nunatak Architectes Sarl
Rte de Branson 45
CH-1926 Fully, Valais
www.nunatak.ch
photos: Dominique Marc Wehrli
/ Francesca Giovanelli (page 115)

ODOS Architects
Darrell O'Donoghue, David Shea
37 Drury Street
IR-Dublin 2
www.odosarchitects.com
photos: Barbara Corsico /
Ros Kavanagh / ODOS architects

Kazuyuki Okumura
Architect
& Associates
4-19-10 Kamirenja-ku,
Mitaka-city, J-Tokio
www.oku-mura.com
photos: Seiichi Osawa

oxen + partner architek-
ten
Kalscheurener Straße 19
D-50354 Hürth-Efferen
www.oxen.de
photos: Stefan Schilling

Peter Kunz Architektur
Neuwiesenstraße 69
CH-8400 Winterthur
www.kunz-architektur.ch
photos: Dominique Marc Wehrli
(page 128 and page 130) /
Valentin Jeck (page 129) / Jürg
Zimmermann (page 131)

Philippe Stuebi
Architekten GmbH
Dipl.-Arch. ETH SIA
mit Eberhard Tröger
Hardstrasse 219
CH-8005 Zurich
www.philippestuebi.ch
photos: Dominique Marc Wehrli

Powerhouse Company
International B.V.
Westzeedijk 399
NL-3024 EK Rotterdam
www.powerhouse-company.
com
photos: Bas Princen

KWK Promes
Robert Konieczny
assistant: Marlena Wolnik,
Lukasz Prazuch
Ul. Rymera 3/5
PL-40-048 Katowice
www.kwkpromes.pl
photos: KWK Promes

Shigeru Ban Architects
America / Dean Maltz
Architect
330 W 38th St. Ste.
USA-811
New York, NY 10018
www.dma-ny.com/
photos: Michael Moran

S.O.F.A. Architekten
Zieglergasse 29/38
A-1070 Vienna
www.sofa-architekten.com
photos: Hertha Hurnaus

Steve Hermann Design
1482 East Valley Road Suite 775
USA-Montecito, CA 93108
www.stevehermanndesign.com
photos: William Macollum

RECOMMENDED LITERATURE

Studio Martin Schroth
Advanced Architectural Design
Herterichweg 50 a
D-91541 Rothenburg o. d.
Tauber
www.martinschroth.de
photos: Jan Döppert / Martin
Schroth (page 156 and page 158
top)

**Sturm und Wartz-
eck GmbH**
Susanne Wartzeck and Jörg
Sturm
Architekten BDA, Innenarchitek-
ten
Wilhelm-Ney-Straße 22
D-36160 Dipperz
www.sturm-wartzeck.de
photos: Jörg Sturm

**Titus Bernhard Architek-
ten**
Gögginger Straße 105 a
D-86199 Augsburg
www.titusbernhardarchitekten.
com
Fotos: Klemens Ortmeyer

Unger & Treina AG
Aargauer Strasse 250
CH-8048 Zürich
www.ungertreina.ch
Fotos: Francesca Giovanelli

- a+u, Nr. 442, 07.2007, edition "Automobile Architecture"
- arch+, Nr. 147, August 1999, edition "Den Tiger reiten. Projekte und
- "Konzepte zur Automobilität" ("Riding the Tiger. Automotive Projects and Concepts")
- archithese, magazine 3.2006, edition "Bauen für das Auto" ("Building for the Car")
- tec21, magazine 21.2006, edition "Auto-Architektur" ("Auto Architecture")
- Wege und Geschichte ("Pathways and History"), magazine 1.2009, edition "Das ruhende Fahrzeug" ("The Resting Vehicle")
- Garage Life, Japan (NEKO Publishing)
- Garage Style Magazine, USA (La Habra CA)
- Carlo Brambilla/Giacomo Cusmano, Progettare e realizzare i parcheggi pubblici e privati, 4. edition, Rimini 2006.
- Edwin Bayer u.a. (publisher), Parkhäuser—aber richtig. Ein Leitfaden für Bauherren, Architekten und Ingenieure, ("Parking Garages—But Well Done. A guideline for builders, architects and engineers")
- 3. edited and expanded edition, Düsseldorf 2006.
- Jonathan Bell, Carchitecture. When The Car And The City Collide, Basel 2001.
- Phil Berg, Ultimate Garages, Minneapolis 2003.
- Phil Berg, Ultimate Garages II, Minneapolis 2007.
- Mark Childs, Parking Spaces. A Design, Implementation, and Use Manual for Architects, Planners, and Engineers, New York 1999.
- Leslie G. Goat, Housing the Horseless Carriage. America's Early Private Garages, in: Perspectives in Vernacular Architecture, Vol. 3, 1989, page 62–72.
- Jürgen Hasse, "Übersehene Räume". Zur Kulturgeschichte und Heterotopologie des Parkhauses, ("Overlooked Rooms". About the Cultural History and Heterotopology of the Parking Garage"), Bielefeld 2007.
- Simon Henley, Parkhaus-Architekturen ("Parking Garage Architecture"), Sulgen 2007.
- Jim Hill, Car Park Designers' Handbook, London 2005.
- Francine Houben, Mobility. A Room with a View, Rotterdam 2003.
- John A. Jakle/Keith A. Sculle, Lots of Parking. Land Use in a Car Culture, Charlottesville VA 2005.
- Philip Jodidio, Architecture and Automobiles, Victoria 2011.
- Britta Jürgs (publisher), Flotte Autos—Schnelle Schlitten. Künstlerinnen & Schriftstellerinnen & ihre Automobile ("Cool Cars—Female Artists and Writers and their Cars"), Berlin 2007.
- Herbert Keck, Auto und Architektur ("Auto and Architecture"), dissertation Technical University Vienna, 1991.
- Herbert Keck, Im Wendekreis des Autos ("The Tropic of Auto"), in: Portal 08, October 2006, page 4–7.
- Uta Keil, Ansgar Oswald, Parkhäuser. Architektur für Automobile ("Parking Garages. Architecture for Automobiles"), Berlin 2008.
- Joachim Kleinmanns, Parkhäuser. Architekturgeschichte einer ungeliebten Notwendigkeit ("Parking Garages. Architectural History of an Unwanted Necessity"), Marburg 2011.
- Marc Kirschbaum, Schöner Parken. Die private Garage als utopischer Raum des Einfamilienhauses ("Better Parking. The Private Garage as the Utopian Space of the Single-Family Home"), in: Hauspark_Parkplatz. Parkhäuser und Parkideen im 21. Jahrhundert ("House Park_Parking Space. Garages and Parking Ideas in the 21. century"), published by the European House for City Culture, Gelsenkirchen 2006, page 24–34.

- Martin Kurz, Garten, Terrasse, Carport. Gestaltung der Außenanlagen leicht gemacht ("Garden, Terrace, Carport. Designing of the Outer Buildings Made Easy"), Taunusstein 2009.
- Llc Home Planners/Connie Brown, Great Garages, Sheds & Outdoor Buildings. 145 Projects you can build, 2. edition., Tucson AZ 2001.
- Floortje Louter/Ed van Savooyen, Parkeren op niveau. De Parkeergarage als Ontwerp Opgave, Bussum 2005.
- Shannon S. McDonald, The Parking Garage. Design and Evolution of a Modern Urban Form, Washington 2007.
- Dirk Meyhöfer, Motortecture. Architektur für Automobilität – Design for Automobility, Ludwigsburg 2003.
- Tony Nourmand (Hg.), Stars & Cars—Prominente und ihre Autos ("Stars & Cars—Celebrities and their Cars"), Berlin 2008.
- Kira Obolensky, Garage. Reinventing the Place We Park, Newton CT 2003.
- Kris Palmer, Dream Garages, Minneapolis 2006.
- Ivo Pauwels, Wooden Dreams: Poolhouses, Carports, Garden Rooms, Guesthouses, Tielt 2011.
- Anton Pech/Günter Warmuth/Klaus Jens/Johannes Zeininger, Parkhäuser—Garagen. Grundlagen, Planung, Betrieb, Reihe Baukonstruktionen ("Parking Places—Garages, Basics, Planning, Maintenance - Building Series"), Vienna 2006.
- Werner Polster/Klaus Voy, Eigenheim und Automobil—Materielle Fundamente der Lebensweise ("Home and Automobile—Material Lifestyle Basics"), in: Klaus Voy/Werner Polster / Claus Thomasberger (publishers), Gesellschaftliche Transformationsprozesse und materielle Lebensweise ("Social Transformation Processes and Material Lifestyle"), Marburg 1991, page 263–315.
- Rex Roy, Motor City Dream Garages, Minneapolis 2007.
- Niklaus Schefer, Philosophie des Automobils. Ästhetik der Bewegung und Kritik des automobilen Designs ("Philosophy of the Automobile. Aesthetic of Movement and Critique of Automotive Design"), Munich 2008.
- Fritz Schmidt jr., Traumgaragen in Deutschland 1.0. Gelebte Träume privater Sammler ("Dream Garages in Germany 1.0. Private Collectors Living their Dreams"), Rüsselsheim 2010.
- Sunset Books (publisher), Carports & Garages, Menlo Park CA 1969.
- Mariarosario Tagliaferri/Marta Serrats (publisher), Parking, Paris 2007.
- Urban Land Institute/National Parking Association, The Dimensions of Parking, 5. edition, Washington 2009.
- Alexander von Vegesack/Mateo Kries (publisher), Automobility—was uns bewegt ("Automobility—What Drives Us"), catalog of the Vitra-Design-Museum, Weil at the Rhine 2003.
- Reimar Zeller (publisher), Das Automobil in der Kunst 1886–1986 ("The Automobile in Art 1886-1986"), Munich 1986.

IMAGE REGISTER